—REGULATIONS—

FINES ARE CHARGED FOR OVERDUE AND/OR LOST LIBRARY MATERIALS; AND, IN ACCORDANCE WITH BOARD POLICY 8741, "GRADES TRANSCRIPTS, DEGREES, AND REGISTRATION PRIVILEGES SHALL BE WITHHELD UNTIL ALL LIBRARY BOOKS OR OTHER LIBRARY MATERIALS ARE RETURNED (TO THE LIBRARY CIRCULATION DESK)."

The Divine Marriage

The Divine Marriage

by

KALIDASA

Translated from the German

of

OTTO WALTER

by

GEORGE BOSWORTH BURCH

Fletcher Professor of Philosophy, Emeritus

Tufts University

LAWRENCE VERRY, INC.

MYSTIC, CONN.

1970

© English Translation Copyrighted 1971, by George Burch.

ISBN No. 0-8426-0180-5

Library of Congress Catalog Card Number: 71-143249

Printed in U.S.A. by
NOBLE OFFSET PRINTERS, INC.
NEW YORK 3, N. Y.

All men and women who recite or sing of this marriage of Uma and Sambhu win the blessings of success in all their works and the joy of a happy wedded life.

— Tulasidasa (Hill's trans., p. 53)

Preface

The divine marriage is the marriage of God and Goddess – but this cannot be said in English. English, like Sanskrit, distinguishes between a *god* (*deva*) in the polytheistic sense and God (*Deva*), written with a capital letter, in the monotheistic sense. Both languages have a feminine of the former, *devi* or *goddess*, but only Sanskrit has a feminine of the latter, *Devi*, which is untranslatable. We speak of the Son of God and the Mother of God but not of the Wife of God. (We can say "the Goddess," but that has a different nuance, being the feminine of "the God," not of "God.") But in Hindu thought everybody should have a wife, even God, or rather especially God, for Goddess is the divine power.

Kalidasa is said to have lived in the fifth century after Christ, although there is no conclusive evidence for that date. His extant works include three plays, two epics, and some shorter poems. The greatest of the plays is *Sakuntala*, widely admired for its delicacy of sentiment; the greater of the epics is the one here translated, equally admirable for its richness of imagination. One is based on legend, the other on myth. In the play the poet presents his image of the perfectly unsophisticated girl; in the epic he presents his image of the perfectly sophisticated one. The play is about Sakuntala, famous, like the

Hebrew Ruth, as ancestress of a royal dynasty. The epic is about the unity of the male and female aspects of deity. This is a central concept of Hindu theology, and its elaboration is an important theme of Hindu mythology. Kalidasa, however, is neither a theologian nor a mythologist but a poet, and it is purely as a poet that he treats the subject.

The Sanskrit title of the poem is *Kumarasambhava*, "Birth of the Prince," usually referred to in English as "Birth of the War-God." The entire work consists of seventeen cantos, of which the last nine describe the conception, birth, and education of the war-god Karttikeya and the battle in which he led the gods to victory over the demon Taraka. Sanskritists generally agree that only the first eight cantos are the genuine work of Kalidasa, the others being additions by some inferior poet. Discussion as to why Kalidasa did not complete the poem, why he stopped writing the "Birth of the Prince" before getting to the prince's birth, is based on the groundless presuppositions that he intended to write a longer epic and that the title given to the expanded poem was its original title. The eight genuine cantos are a complete work with perfect artistic unity. The mythological and moral significance of the war-god as motivating the marriage is essential to the story, but his subsequent career is of secondary interest.

English versions known to me are completely lacking in literary value, and none includes all eight cantos, except a very crude anonymous translation published at Calcutta in 1901. The German version by Otto Walter, published in 1913, is far superior. The present work is a translation of this. The unit of Sanskrit epic poetry is the couplet of two verses presenting a single thought, represented here, as in the German, by a prose paragraph. The notes are mainly aids for readers not acquainted with Hindu mythology. There are doubtless philosophical, allegorical, and hidden meanings in the poem, but it is not the function of a translator to discover these. It is hoped that, pending the making of a competent translation directly from the Sanskrit, this version may serve to acquaint English-speaking readers with one of the finest works of Sanskrit literature.

I am indebted to Dr. Alice Angyal for a critical comparison of the text with its German original.

G.B.B.

Table of Contents

The Divine Marriage

Canto 1
Rebirth of the Goddess

Far in the North the divine King of Mountains, Himalaya, towers aloft. Washed in the eastern and western oceans, he stands there like a measuring-rod of the earth.

According to an ancient myth, all the other mountains, regarding him as a calf, drew forth from the earth, over which King Prithu then ruled, brilliant jewels and great phosphorescent herbs, as if she were a cow giving milk, the golden mountain Meru being the skillful milker.

He is an inexhaustible source of precious stones, nor does the snow diminish this intrinsic beauty of his, for a single flaw is lost in the multitude of good properties, as the dark spot is lost in the radiance of the moon.

His peaks are laden with bloodstone. When the ruddy glare from this mineral is reflected on wisps of clouds, it appears to be a sunset, and so leads the celestial nymphs[1] to adorn their bodies for coquetry and hurry to the evening dance, which, in their amorous absentmindedness, they think is about to take place.

At the foot of the mountain the holy men refresh themselves in the shade of the clouds which wander over the slopes of his valleys. Then, however, aroused by sudden showers, they betake themselves to his sunny peaks.

The hunter folk who dwell on the mountain follow the track of elephant-killing lions by the pearls[2] which drop from their claws and betray it, even when their footprints can no longer be recognized, the blood being washed away by the melting snow.

His birchbark, on which words are written with a red fluid, so that they shine like the red drops on an elephant's hide, serve the elfin maidens for love letters.

By the whistling of the wind blowing out from the mouth of his caves and filling the hollows of the reeds the mountain seems to try to sound the keynote for the singing of the satyrs.

His ridges are fragrant with the scent rising from the milky sap of the pine trees, against which the elephants rub themselves to relieve the intolerable itching of their cheeks.

There the herbs, which fill the recesses of the cave dwellings with their phosphorescence, serve the woodsmen and their wives as lamps, which illumine their lovemaking but never need to be filled with oil.

[11]   Even when the path they follow hurts their toes and heels with hailstones, the goblin women do not change their slow pace, for the burden of their hips and breasts, which they can hardly carry, prevents their going faster.

The gloom abiding in his caves shies like the owl at break of day, but it is protected from the sun-god by the mountain. Even a person of lowly origin, when a suppliant at the homes of the magnanimous, receives such consideration as otherwise only a noble man would deserve to enjoy.

The heifer yaks lend a true significance to his title "King of Mountains" by their fly-brush tails,[3] the brilliance of which shines forth in all directions as they are tossed back and forth on both sides, shining white as moonlight.

There clouds circling and clinging about the entries of the cave dwellings form veils for the modest goblin maidens when they take off their clothes.

His wind, laden with drops of water from the falls of the Ganges, shakes many a fragrant pine tree, ruffles the peacock feathers on the hunters' belts, and is greeted with joy by these mountain dwellers as they pursue the gazelle.

The sun-god, revolving along his path below, shoots his rays upward to wake the lotus blossoms, the residue of those plucked by the hand of the Seven Wise Seers, growing in the ponds on his heights.

Now when the Creator took into consideration that this mountain was the source of the material of sacrifice,[4] and also recognized his might, which seemed capable of carrying the earth, he gave him personally both a share in the sacrifices and the power of kingship over all other mountains.

Himalaya, however, a friend of Mount Meru and an observer of duty, took Mena to himself as consort, in accordance with law, in order to assure the perpetuation of his race. She was a maiden begotten from the spirit of the Fathers, an object of reverence even for the sages, but for him a worthy wife.

In due time, when they had enjoyed such lovemaking as accorded with her beauty, the mountain monarch's bride, in the bloom of ravishing youth, became pregnant.

She gave birth to a son, Mainaka, whom later the serpent maidens loved, who contracted a bond of friendship with the ocean, and who avoided the pain of the lightning wound when Indra seized by rage clipped off the wings of the mountains.

And now the Pure Female Being,[5] Daksha's daughter, *[21]* Siva's former wife, who provoked by her father's offence[6] had abandoned her body through yoga, came to the mountain's wife to be reincarnated in her.

The beautiful one was now begotten, by the King of Mountains, in his devout wife, as welfare is begotten, by perserverance, in good conduct which never goes astray.

The day when she entered the world, on which every

quarter of the sky shone clear, the wind was free from dust, and a shower of flowers fell from heaven accompanied by a blowing of conches, was a blessing for all creation, animate and inanimate.

With this daughter, who was surrounded by the bright light of a halo, the mother was more radiant even than the slope of Mount Vidura in Ceylon when it glitters with the fragment of a precious stone broken off by the thunder of newly gathered clouds.

Day by day, after coming to the world, the girl grew more and more, and her beautiful limbs waxed like the moon, which, after its crescent has appeared, keeps growing bigger every day until all its parts are bright with light.

By her relatives, whose darling she was, she was named Parvati, because she was of the race of a mountain. Later, however, the pretty girl was always called Uma, because her mother was constantly restraining her from some austerity by crying "U ma" (Oh don't).

Although the mountain had many offspring, his eyes were never satiated with this child. Although the spring has an infinite variety of flowers, the swarm of bees clings close to the mango blossom.

As a lamp by its brightly shining flame, as the path of heaven by its triple water-course, and as a scholar by words formed with grammatical correctness obtain purification and ornamentation, so Himalaya by this maid was both purified and adorned.

In her childhood she exhausted the delights of play, loving to amuse herself with her balls and dolls in the company of her playmates on the terraces which she built on the sandy banks of the Ganges.

As in autumn to the Ganges come the flocks of swans, as at night to the herb comes its own phosphorescence, so to this girl so eager for learning, when the time for education arrived, came all the knowledge acquired in her former existence.

But when she entered upon the period of life which [31] follows childhood, this age became an ornament of her tender body without art, a cause of intoxication without wine, and a weapon of Kama,[7] but without flowers.

As a painting unfolds under the brush and the water lily blossoms in beauty under the sunshine, so her body developed fully under her blooming youth and attained a beauty equally perfect in every part.

Her two feet, which seemed to exhale redness by the luster of the nails of the great toes, held high as she trod the ground, assumed the beauty of a freely swaying hibiscus flower.

As she walked along, stooping, with lovely mincing steps, one would have thought that she had been instructed by the royal swans, who longed for instruction in return and would gladly have possessed the tinkling of her anklets.

The Creator, who formed her feet beautiful, symmetrical, rounded, and not too long, took great pains, as it were, with this beauty, which was still to be formed in her other limbs.

Although the trunk of the lordly elephant and the exquisite stem of the banana tree have a popular reputation for great beauty, yet they could never serve as objects of comparison for her legs, for the skin of the trunk is rough, and the banana tree is always cool.

Were not the flawless young girl's splendid hips already so broad that she might later be taken by Siva on his lap, which no other woman might aspire to?

The fine rows of her youthful body down, which penetrated into her deep navel and ran out beyond her loin cloth, seemed like the gleam of the dark jewel which glittered in the middle of her belt.

The maiden, whose waist was like an hourglass,[8] had three beautiful folds in the middle of her body. These had been formed there by her blooming youth as if steps for the god of love to climb on.

The fair breasts of this girl, who gazed around with eyes

like water lilies, touched each other and were so developed that not once did the filaments of a lotus stalk find room between the two, adorned with dark nipples.

[41]   Her two hands were so resplendent with their bright fingernails that they put the budding asoka leaf to shame, and in the evening they made the brilliance of the sky, shining with the disk of the newly risen moon, seem unnecessary.

I believe that her two arms were more delicate even than the acacia flower, for the god who bears the dolphin on his banner[9] had destined them to become a noose for Siva's neck, in spite of his own destruction.

As her bosom rose and fell, her pearl necklace shed round her throat a light it lent and also borrowed, for each reflected the other's brilliance.

When fickle Beauty goes to the moon, she no longer enjoys the lotus blossom's form,[10] or if she comes to this, she cannot rejoice in the loveliness of the moon. In Uma's face, however, she found twofold delight, for there she saw lotus and moon together.

If a blossom were on a young branch and a pearl on a bed of coral, they would resemble her merry smile as it brightened her two red lips.

When the maid began to talk, speaking sweetly with a voice dripping with nectar, even the cuckoo's song would jar the hearer like a harp string out of tune when it is touched.

Did the maiden with her big eyes learn from the gazelles that glance which wandered here and there like a lotus blossom swaying in the wind, or did they learn it from Parvati?

Hardly had the god of love seen the loveliness of her two eyebrows, marked by long lines, curved as if by a pencil with collyrium, dexterous in flirtation, when he gave up all pride in the splendor of his bow.

If a feeling of shame could rule the hearts of animals, the heifer yaks would surely find their own tails less dear to them on seeing the mountain princess's long hair.

The Creator carefully formed this maid with the wealth of all objects which could serve for comparisons, and which found their proper places in her, as if he had intended to exhibit all beauty in one spot.

When the wise seer Narada, who moves over the world at will, once saw her at her father's home, he prophesied, "She alone will be the bride of Siva[11] and will become one flesh with him through love." [51]

Therefore, although she was already a mature maiden, her father showed no desire for any other suitor, for no other fires but Agni enjoy the sacrifices consecrated with sacred words.

The mountain could not offer his daughter in marriage to the God of gods, when he had not sued for her. A gentleman assumes indifference from fear that his petition may be rejected, even though its object is desired.

The pearly-toothed Goddess had once, in a former existence in this world, abandoned her body in distress at Daksha's scorn. Since that time Siva was living without a wife, free from every contact with things of sense.

On one of Himalaya's mountain slopes, where sweet smelling pine trees were sprinkled by the falls of the Ganges, the fragrance of musk filled the air, and the songs of the satyrs were heard, he took up his abode, his heart wrapped up in a longing for asceticism, his body in a hide, his soul in meditation.

The hosts of his attendants sat upon rocks, which emitted an odor of pitch. They were beautifully decorated with red arsenic, wild olive branches hung down from their ears, and birchbark, pleasant to the touch, formed their garments.

His steed, the white bull, tore up the surface of the glaciers with his sharp hoofs. The lovely sound of his voice rang out with pride. The terrified wild oxen scarcely dared look at him. He bellowed loudly, for he could not endure the roars resounding from the throats of the lions.

Meanwhile the eight-formed God had kindled a fire

(another form of himself) and was performing works of asceticism there, seeking some fruit of asceticism, although himself the distributor of its rewards.

He, the inestimable God, who is glorified by all the host of heaven, was now honored with many offerings by the Lord of Mountains, who appointed his devout daughter to serve him, together with her two companions.

Siva permitted her to do so because she was of service to him, although she was an enemy to his pious meditation. They are truly imperturbable whose minds are not perturbed even when a cause of perturbation appears.

[61]   And now the maid, resplendent with her beautiful hair, brought her offerings to Siva every day. She picked flowers for the sacrifice, showed herself skillful in scouring the altar, and fetched water and kusha grass as needed for the sacred rites, and her consequent fatigue was relieved by the moonbeams shining on his head.

Canto 2
Appeal of the Gods

While this was going on, the gods, oppressed by the demon Taraka, betook themselves to the house of Brahma,[12] with Indra at their head.

And now Brahma revealed himself in person before them, whose faces had lost their former radiance, like the sun-god showing himself to the ponds where the lotus flowers are sleeping.

They bowed low before him, Creator of the universe, the four-faced God, Lord of all wisdom, and glorified him with the following profound words:

"Glory be to thee, thou triune God! Thou wast absolute Oneness until the creation was accomplished. Thou didst divide thyself into the three qualities, and thus received thy various names.

"In the beginning thou, thyself unbegotten, impregnated the waters with thy seed, and not without fruit, for from it has arisen the All, the animate and the inanimate, and as the source of all thou art glorified in song.

"Thou hast shown thy power in three forms.[13] Thou alone art the ground of the creation of this world, and also the cause of its continued preservation and final dissolution.

"Male and Female were derived from thee as parts of

9

thyself, when thou didst split thy body in two, in order to procreate. They are called the parents of creation, which continues to multiply.

"Thou dividest day and night according to thy own measure of time. When thou sleepest, all beings die; when thou wakest, they rise again.

"Thou art the cause of this world, thyself uncaused. Thou settest the end of the world, thyself unending. Thou art the beginning of the world, thyself eternal. Thou art the lord of this world, thyself without a peer.

"Thou knowest thy own being by thy own self. Thou createst thyself, and thou absorbest thyself again into thyself.

/11/   "Thou art the fluid and the firm solid, the big and the little, the light and the heavy, thou art the revealed and the hidden. Thou art able to enter into other bodies according to thy will.

"Thou alone art the only source of the holy Vedas, which begin with "Aum," are chanted in three accents, are manifested outwardly in sacrifices, but rewarded spiritually by salvation.

"Thou art called Matter, which sets a boundary to the soul. Thou art known as Spirit, which sees Matter, yet is independent of it.

"Thou art the Father of all fathers, the God of the gods. Thou standest higher than the highest. Thou art the source of all creators.

"Thou art the sacrifice, and thou the sacrificer. Thou art that which is to be enjoyed, but also he who enjoys it. Thou art that which is to be known, thou the knower; the thinker, and also the supreme object of thought."

When the Creator had heard this true eulogy, which pleased him and made him gracious, he replied to the assembled gods.

The words which flowed from the fourfold mouth of the

Primeval Sage fulfilled their purpose perfectly, because they observed the four categories of logic.

"Welcome to me, O powers, ye who have come to me all together, and done your homage with your mighty yoke-like arms.

"How does it happen that your former brilliance no longer makes you radiant? Your countenances are all like stars when a snowstorm stops their shining.

"Indra no longer brandishes his thunderbolt, that weapon of the gods. Its flashes have ceased, and its points seem blunt to me.

"Oh tell me, why has that noose become so slack, which Varuna[14] holds in his hand and which no enemy can withstand? It is like a serpent whose strength has been destroyed by a charm. *[21]*

"Kuvera's[15] arm, like a tree with a branch broken off, no longer carries its club. It proclaims, as it were, his disgrace, and is like an arrow in the heart.

"Even Yama[16] lets his tarnished staff trail on the ground. It used to reach its goal, but now it seems powerless, like an extinguished firebrand.

"Why are the gods of light so cold? Their fire is extinguished. They seem to me as if painted in a picture, that one can look at as he will.

"Confusion reigns, from which I gather that the wind-gods have been checked in their course. One infers that the river has been obstructed when it flows backward.

"The storm-gods are no longer howling. Their hair hangs down, and their horns droop.

"Have you now surrendered the lofty places where you used to dwell to more powerful enemies, like general rules forced to yield to particular exceptions?

"Tell me therefore, Beloved, what you wish of me in

coming here. On me depends the world's creation; on you, its protection."

Then Indra, with all his thousand eyes, sparkling like a pond of lotuses swaying in a gentle breeze, looked at his counselor.

He, the Lord of Eloquence, Indra's two-eyed eye, who sees with them more even than Indra with his thousand, now spoke to Brahma as follows, joining his hands.

[31]   "Holy One, what thou hast said is only too true. Those lofty places which we attained the enemy possesses. Why, O Lord, is this not known to thee, since thou dwellest in every being?

"The great demon Taraka, exalted by thy favor, is shining like a comet, an evil omen for the world.

"In his city, the sun-god spreads his warmth only enough to open the blossoms of the lotus flowers on his ponds.

"To him the moon-god does homage with all his parts all the time, save only the crescent which forms Siva's diadem.

"In his pleasure garden, the wind stops its motion, fearing to carry off the flowers there, and blows as gently as a palm-leaf fan.

"The seasons have given up their regular course. They think only of blossom time for him, and serve him like watchmen in a hermitage.

"The sea can hardly wait for the time when the pearls will have grown in its depths, to serve as offerings for him.

"At night the serpent-spirits, Vasuki at their head, do homage to him with the flashing light shining from their crest gems. Thus they furnish lamps for him, which last forever and never go out.

"Indra, mindful of the favors granted him, frequently courts him with garlands from the wishing-trees, which he sends to him by envoys.

"Although he is propitiated in all these ways, nevertheless he still oppresses the three worlds. An evil man is checked only when evil is done to him in return, never by returning good for evil.

"He has caused the trees of paradise, whose branches used   /41/
to be bent gently by the hands of the goddesses, to be broken
to pieces and torn down.

"When he lies asleep, he is fanned by captive goddesses.
The breezes of the fans are like sighs, and moistened with
teardrops.

"He tears off the peaks of Mount Meru, where the
sun-god's coursers used to stamp their hoofs, to make pleasure
hills from them in his own palatial home.

"The waters of the Ganges are made turbid by the
secretions of celestial elephants, the ponds have now become
their stalls, and golden lotus blossoms serve as fodder for them.

"The road formerly enlivened by the chariots of the gods
is deserted, for assault by him is everywhere feared, and so the
vista of the three worlds no longer gives pleasure to the gods.

"This wily demon snatches from the fire-god's mouth,
before our eyes, the offerings which the priest is consecrating at
the sacrifices.

"He has stolen Uchchaihsravas, that jewel of a horse, as
an incarnation of the glory already won from Indra.

"All our efforts against this evil are futile, just as even
powerful medicines are of no avail in the case of a disease in
which the three humors have combined.

"Vishnu's discus, which gives out sparks at its impact and
was formerly our hope of victory, he has hung round his neck
as an ornament to wear on his breast.

"His elephants have defeated Airavata[17] in battle, and
now play the game of striking the bank with the stormclouds.

"Therefore we wish to have a general created for the   /51/
overthrow of this demon, like yogis establishing a vanguard of
virtue, whereby the chains of their former deeds are broken and
rebirth escaped forever.

"May Indra place him at our head as champion of the

host of gods! Then will he bring back to us the goddess of victory from the side of the enemy, who now holds her as if a prisoner of war."

After this discourse Brahma himself made a speech which surpassed in felicitousness the rain which follows a clap of thunder.

"Your wish shall be fulfilled. Only have patience. I myself, however, will not beget the general through whom success will come.

"This demon holds his power from me. Therefore he shall not owe his downfall also to me. One ought not to chop down with an ax even a venomous tree which he himself has grown.

"He chose all this himself, and I promised it to him, for this boon which I granted him extinguished his ardor, which might have produced a universal conflagration.

"Who else can offer resistance to this fierce warrior when roused to action, save only the seed of the black-necked, red-haired God?[18]

"For this God is the Supreme Light beyond the bounds of darkness. Neither I nor Vishnu can comprehend the fullness of his might.

"You must now attract the heart of Siva, who is plunged in serene meditation, by the charm of Uma's beauty, as one allures the iron by the magnet.

"Only these two, Uma and the Waters, can ever bear the force of the seed ejected by Siva and by me.

[61]   "When the son of this black-necked God becomes your general, he will soon display his strength, and will loosen the braided tresses of the captive goddesses."

When Brahma had thus spoken to the gods, he vanished. But they fixed their minds on their duties and hastened back to heaven again.

There, however, Indra bethought him of Kama, and then went to him in spirit with redoubled speed, for haste was necessary if the affair was to be successful.

The god of love was just hanging his bow, the tips of which were a match for the creeper-like eyebrows of a beautiful woman, around his neck, which showed the marks of the goddess Rati's bracelets, and was putting green mango shoots into the hands of his friend, the Spring. He immediately stood before Indra, respectfully joining his hands.

Canto 3
Death of Love

$\mathcal{I}$ndra's thousand eyes fell all at once upon this god, as if they had forgotten the other gods. Great lords customarily turn to various subordinates when they desire some service.

Taking a seat which Indra offered him, saying, "Sit down here beside my throne," Kama gladly accepted his lord's favor, bowing his head, and began to speak to him privately.

"Knowing as thou dost the various ways of mankind, tell me now what thou desirest to have done in the worlds. I wish the mark of favor, which thy thinking of me has bestowed upon me, to be increased still more by some command which thou wilt give me.

"Who is it, who through excessive asceticism is striving for a lofty place and has aroused thy envy? Name him to me, so that he may become submissive to my bow, on which I have placed an arrow.

"Who, without thy approval, has trod the way of emancipation from fear of being reborn again? For a long time he shall remain there, chained by the sideward glances of beautiful women looking lovely with contracted eyebrows.

"Tell me, to which of thy enemies shall I send Passion as my envoy to annihilate both his virtues and his worldly success, as the high flood destroys both banks of the river, even though Ushanas[19] may have instructed him in all worldly wisdom?

"What married woman, who has vowed to love faithfully

a single husband, but who has found an entrance into thy fickle heart by her charm, dost thou wish to have forget all shame and impulsively throw her arms around thy neck?

"Say, O ardent lover, before what beautiful woman hast thou prostrated thyself after a lovers' quarrel, only to be spurned in anger? I will make her tormented body seek repose on a bed of fresh leaves.

"Be gracious, Lord. Let thy weapon rest. Who verily exists among all the enemies of the gods who cannot be made to lose his strength by means of my arrows and to tremble before mere women, when their lips quiver with anger?

"Although I use only flowers for weapons, I would be able, with thy leave, to destroy the strength of Siva himself, with his mace in his hand, if I might choose Spring as a single companion. Say, are there any other archers in the world like me?"

Then Indra let his feet drop from his thighs to the footstool, sanctifying it by his touch, and spoke as follows to the god of love, who was showing his fitness for the task at hand.   *[11]*

"All this is possible for thee, my friend. The thunderbolt and thou are at my service as my two weapons. The former, indeed, is blunt against such as have waxed mighty through the power of their asceticism, but thou, the other weapon, dost penetrate everywhere and dost attain thy goal.

"I know thy powers. That is why I shall assign a difficult work to thee. Thou art my equal. God Krishna appointed the Sesha serpent to bear him up because he held him capable of supporting the earth with his body.

"Thy extolling of thy arrow's power to make its way to Siva has already brought our work near to its goal. Know, then, that this is just what all the gods desire, oppressed as they are by powerful foes.

"For the gods desire to have a son of Siva's might to be their general, and so through him to bear away the victory. The

God, however, who might be overcome by the fall of a single one of thy arrows, has completely plunged himself in Brahman, and touches the sacred spots of the body as he recites sacred mantras.

"Let him, the Self-Controlled, take his pleasure in the pious daughter of the Mountain of Snow. 'She alone of all women is capable of receiving Siva's seed in herself,' Brahma himself has revealed to us.

" 'Obedient to her father's command, the mountain princess is doing homage to the God Siva, who is devoting himself to asceticism on a lofty plateau.' Thus have I heard from the mouth of the nymphs, for that race serve me as my spies.

"Go, therefore, and accomplish the work of the gods, so that we may see its success. This affair will attain its end only through another as a means, but requires thee as its ultimate cause, as the seed needs water before it can sprout.

"None other better than thou can guide the flight of the arrow toward this God, who shall accomplish the victory of the gods. Thou art already successful. A task which no others dare to undertake brings glory to men even when it is not yet completed.

"The gods here are the petitioners, and it is the business of the three worlds. The work pertains to thy bow alone, and it is not too cruel. Thou hast enviable powers which amaze us all.

/21/   "Spring, Kama, is closely allied to thee, and so thy companion, without special command. Who, pray, ever commands the wind to blow the fire into a blaze?"

With the words, "So be it," the god of love accepted his lord's commission as if raising to his head a garland of flowers presented at the end of a religious ceremony. Then he hastily prepared himself for the trip. As he started out, Indra touched his body with his own hand, which had become very rough from frequently striking the elephant Airavata.

Resolved upon the successful outcome of this work even

at the sacrifice of his own life, accompanied by his dear friend Spring and his wife the goddess Rati, with foreboding of the tragedy to come, he went to the hermitage situated in the Himalaya Mountains where Siva was performing his ascetic devotions.

And now Spring came down upon this forest and displayed himself in his visible form,[20] the pride of the god of love, but an impediment to the ascetic meditation of serene hermits.

When the sun-god's time for tarrying in the South had passed, and he had begun to wend his way toward the quarter of heaven protected by god Kuvera,[21] the breeze of the southern quarter was like a sigh of grief uttered by a faithful wife when her husband, burning with lust, ignores the time for lovemaking with her and hurries to some beauty protected by a monster.

All at once the asoka tree covered itself with flowers and new leaves from trunk to twigs, not waiting for women with tinkling anklets to touch it with their feet.[22]

Hardly had the budding mango flower arrow burst into blossom, the leaves on its stem forming beautiful feathers, when Spring set the bees upon it, as if to be the signature of the god of love.[23]

Although the karnikara flower was the most gorgeous in color, it filled the soul with disappointment because it had no fragrance. The Creator does not ordinarily bestow all good properties upon one thing.

The buds of the wingseed, brilliantly red and curved like the new moon, not yet having opened, shone red like scratches of nails inflicted by Spring as he caressed the face of the forest.

The goddess of spring adorned her brow with the tilaka,[24] shining brightly above the black lines of the eybrow pencil (closely clinging bees provided these), and painted her lips (the mango boughs) with a rouge which shone as delicately as the rising sun.

[31]   Through woods where leaves fell rustling down ran
gazelles, agitated by the intoxication of love, and filling their
eyes with priyala pollen when they ran against the wind.

The cuckoo's throat glittered with a ruddy sheen, because
he had been tasting of the mango shoot. His sweet song became
the voice of Love, designed to put an end to the pouting of
proud women.

The goblin women began to perspire; their tilakas began
to run. Winter now being past, their lips shone clearly again,[25]
and their countenances seemed fairer.

When the ascetics whose huts stood in Siva's forest
noticed the signs of spring, coming much too early, they were
scarcely able to subdue their senses, the movements of which
they restrained with difficulty.

Then Kama arrived in this region with the goddess Rati
and his flowery bow, already strung, and all at once every
couple let their love, which had now reached its highest point,
show itself in their behavior.

The bee followed his sweetheart and sipped the nectar
from the same blossom as she. The black antelope scratched his
doe with his horn, while she closed her eyes at the touch.

The female elephant lovingly sprayed her mate with a
trunkful of water, fragrant with lotus flower filaments. The
drake offered his beloved a half eaten lotus stem.

Whenever a pause arose during the singing, the goblin
would kiss his sweetheart's face, the paint on which was partly
washed off by drops of perspiration. Her eyes, however, would
glitter and roll, for she had already tasted of the nectar wine.

Even the trees received the entwining embraces of their
wives, the creepers, round their bending boughs. In place of
breasts they offered rounded clusters of flowers; in place of lips,
their shimmering tendrils.

Although at this moment Siva became aware of the song
of the nymphs, still he remained serene in his meditation.

Disturbances never hinder the zeal of those who have mastered themselves.

His doorkeeper, named Nandi, stood at the entrance of the creeper hut, with his golden staff resting on his left forearm, and prevented Siva's hosts from approaching. He did it by the command of a finger laid on his lips, with the words, "Let there be no levity." [41]

Immediately thereupon the trees stood motionless, the humming of the bees ceased, the birds were silent, the gazelles no more sprang back and forth. Thus, at the guard's command, the whole forest suddenly seemed perfectly still, like a painted picture.

God Kama, however, avoided Nandi's sight, as a traveler avoids that part of the sky where Venus[26] shines before his face, and entered Siva's place of meditation, at the sides of which the olive trees let their branches droop to the ground.

There, as his doom approached, he saw the three-eyed God in the midst of his asceticism, sitting on a bench of sweet-smelling pine wood covered with a tigerskin.

His body was held erect and motionless, one leg was crossed over the other, both shoulders were stooped, and the palms of his hands were up, so that a full blown lotus seemed to be growing in his lap.

His tufts of hair were bound up with serpents, a double rosary hung down from his ear, and his gnarled garment, made of the hide of a black antelope, shone even darker where it mingled its gleam with that of his throat.

His eyes, serene, awful, almost closed, directed their glance downward to his nose. His eyebrows were not contracted, his eyelashes were motionless.

Like a cloud without rainstorms, like a pond without waves, like a quiet flame not blown by any wind — such was God Siva, as he held his breath.

The beauty of the crescent moon, shining more delicately

than a lotus blossom filament, was entirely obscured by the rays of light which shone brilliantly from his head, shooting forth from the orifice of the third eye on his forehead.

His soul, held far from the nine gateways, rested in his heart, where it pursued its meditation, until it contemplated in its own self the Universal Spirit, which the wise call eternal.

[51]   The god of love, his hands trembling with fear, thus observed Siva, who cannot be conquered even in thought, from close by, nor did he notice that the bow and arrow had already dropped from his hand.

Suddenly the mountain princess appeared before the bower followed by wood nymphs, and the beauty of her body gave new life, as it were, to Kama's well nigh exhausted strength.

Her body was adorned with spring flowers, of which the asoka blossom put the ruby to shame, the karnikara blossom shone brighter than gold, and the sindhuvara might have served her as a string of pearls.

Stooping a little under the weight of her rounded breasts and clad in a crimson robe which shone like the rising sun, the maiden seemed like a creeper with new shoots, bent down, as it moves along, under its rounded clusters of blossoms.

She was holding up her belt, a beautifully woven garland of monkeyface flowers, which kept slipping down from her waist, to become, as it were, another bowstring for the god of love, deposited by him in that most fitting place.

With a lotus blossom, which she carried as a plaything, she kept beating off a bee, which buzzed around her rosy lips, its desire excited by the fragrance of her breath, while her eyes kept looking around in fright.[27]

The bearer of the flowery bow had scarcely seen the damsel, flawless in every limb, who put to shame even goddess Rati, when his hope was revived of attaining success in his design against the self-restrained Siva.

As Uma approached the door of Siva, her future

bridegroom, the God, who was now contemplating in his own soul that Light which is called the Supreme Spirit, came out of his trance.

He gradually let out his breath and then relaxed his fixed, cross-legged posture, so that the great serpent on the ground below could scarcely keep its position by means of its pointed hoods.

The doorkeeper Nandi, however, prostrated himself before him and announced, "The mountain princess has approached to bring thee her homage." Thereupon he let her enter, as Siva permitted by a mere motion of the eybrows.

Then her companions bowed down and scattered before *[61]* Siva's feet the spring flowers they had picked, mingled with creeper tendrils.

Parvati also bowed her head before Siva, so that the still dewy karnikara blossom shining brightly in her black locks fell to the ground, and the spray of flowers dropped from her ear.

"May thou obtain a husband who enjoys no other wife." He addressed her with these words, in which he revealed the exact truth, for never in the world do the words of great personages give a false meaning.

Kama, however, like a moth about to fly into a flame, observing that the propitious moment for his arrow had come, took his place at Uma's side, readjusted the bowstring, and aimed at God Siva.

Meanwhile Parvati's rosy hand was offering a rosary to the ascetic Siva. She had made it herself out of seeds of lotus flowers from the Ganges, and had dried it in the sun.

Scarcely had he approached her in order to accept it, for worshipers always pleased him, when the god of love laid on his bow a never-failing arrow, named Fascination.

And now Siva looked into Uma's face with its bright red lips. His serenity was only slightly ruffled, like the sea at moonrise.

She, on the other hand, revealed her passion for him by

her limbs, which were like tender, opening kadamba blossoms.[28] Thus she remained standing before him, with averted face, looking perfectly ravishing as her eyes moved back and forth.

In a moment the God had overcome the movement of his senses. Restraining them, he looked toward the horizon in every direction to discover the cause of his perturbation.

And there he saw Kama, his fist against the outer corner of his right eye, his shoulders stooped, his left knee bent, his bow drawn into a semicircle, on the point of shooting him.

[71]   His rage aroused by this assault on his asceticism, a terrifying scowl covered his face, and suddenly a flash of fire shot out from his third eye.

And as the welkin rang with the cries of the gods, "Stop thy rage, stop, O Master!" the flame streaming from Siva's eye reduced the god of love to a heap of ashes.

The goddess Rati swooned at this utter disaster, and all her senses came to a standstill, but this was a blessing for her, since for a moment she did not know of her lord's death.

When the ascetic Siva had thus instantly annihilated this disturber of his meditation, as a thunderbolt shatters a tree, he vanished, along with his hosts, to tarry no longer in the vicinity of a girl.

And when the daughter of the mountain saw that her lofty father's desire and intention, as well as her own beauty, had been made vain, overcome with shame at the thought, "It happened before the eyes of my best friends," she could scarcely make her way homeward in despair.

The mountain, however, came running to his daughter, who aroused pity and had closed her eyes in fear of Siva's wrath, took her in his arms, and hurried along the path as fast as he could run, like a celestial elephant with a lotus blossom between its tusks.

Canto 4
Lament for Love

Whereupon Rati, who had fallen in a faint, no longer mistress of her limbs, was awakened from her swoon by Destiny, bringing her to youthful widowhood with its intolerable sorrow.

As her eyes opened at the end of her swoon, she looked all around, not knowing that those eyes, which searched so futilely, would never again behold the darling of her heart.

"Art thou alive, O prince of my life?" she cried, and was about to get up from the ground again, when right before her she saw a heap of ashes in the form of a man lying on the earth, produced by Siva's fiery wrath.

Then she gave way to grief, tearing her hair, embracing the earth, discoloring her breasts with dust. Her cries resounded through the sylvan dale, so that it too seemed to be held in the grip of sorrow.

"Thy body, which was so graceful that lovers always chose it for comparisons, is now transformed like this, and I have not torn myself apart? Oh, women are hard-hearted!

"Why hast thou forsaken me, when my whole life depended on thee? In a single moment thou hast broken the bond of our friendship and turned away from me, like the water of a flooded pond which breaks through the dike and flows away, leaving behind the lotus flower whose life was dependent on it.

"Never wast thou unloving to me, and thou knowest that I gave thee nothing but love. Why, then, without any reason dost thou now deprive Rati of thy sight, when she is calling for thee?

"Art thou thinking, Kama, of that time when I bound thee fast with my belt, because I heard thee speak some strange name? Art thou thinking of how I beat thee with the lotus flower which had been hanging from my ear, so that thy eyes were filled with pollen dropping from the blossom?

"Those words so dear to me, which I received from thee, 'Thou alone dwellest in my heart,' must have been a deception. If they were not mere words of flattery, why then has thy body gone away? Why is Rati still here quite unhurt?

"Thou hast hardly reached the other world, yet I will follow thy steps. Fate has cheated this world. Surely the happiness of all earthly beings is derived from thee alone.

[11]   "When night has veiled the city streets in darkness, who but thee, beloved, can guide the steps of girls, trembling with fear of the thunder, to their lovers' homes?

"The intoxication of women, caused by drinking wine, which makes their reddened eyes roll and interrupts their speech at every word, now seems fruitless without thee.

"When the moon hears that his dearest friend's body has become a memory, he will have no more reason for rising. When the time for waning has passed, dear spirit, he will shed the light of his slender crescent only sorrowfully.

"The budding mango shoot, radiant with the orange splendor of its petals and hailed by the lovely song of the cuckoo—whose arrow will it be now, for shooting men?

"This row of black bees, which often served thee as a bowstring, moans with me in my heavy grief by its humming, like a mournful dirge.

"Assume thy lovely form again, rise up, and then say to the cuckoo's mate, who can utter her call so lovingly, 'Be now again my messenger of love.'

"When I think of how thou wouldst beseech me, bow thy head, fall at my feet, hug me, how I would quiver, how we would enjoy the secret delights of love — oh, every bit of peace flees from my breast.

"O master of all the arts of love, this garland of spring flowers which thou thyself bound round my waist is still fresh, but thy handsome form has disappeared.

"Thou must dye my left foot here, for the dyeing was not finished when the cruel gods thought of thee and snatched thee away from here. Oh, come back to me!

"I will hasten to thee in the way of a moth,[29] and then once more I will lie on thy bosom, my darling, before the goddesses in heaven, skilled as they are in flirtation, begin to look at thee with their amorous glances.

"Even though I follow after thee, my beloved, it will still *[21]* be said to my shame that Rati remained living even for a moment when she was separated from god Kama.

"Thou art summoned to the other world, but how shall I adorn thy body for its last rites? Life and body both have been taken away, all unexpectedly.

"I still remember how thou used to make thy arrow straight, how thy bow used to lie in thy lap, how thou used to talk and laugh with Spring, and would glance at me out of the corner of thy eye.

"Where has Spring gone now, thy dear friend, who furnished thy bow with flowers? Did not the Archer God, in his great rage, send him also to follow the path of his friend?"

Then Spring appeared in person, wounded by her lamenting words as by poisoned arrows in his heart, to console the sorrow-stricken goddess.

When she saw him, she began to weep bitterly and beat her bosom, which her breasts completely covered. Truly, grief breaks out as if through an open gate when we see before our eyes the dear ones who are near to us.

Sobbing with sorrow she spoke. "O Spring, what is left to

thee now of thy dear comrade? Ashes — look! Gray as a dove, they are now being scattered all around by the winds, in tiny particles.

"O Kama, show thyself again! Spring is longing for thee. A man's love for his wife may not be enduring, but his love for his friend is.

"He was so near to thee! Was not he the agent who made the whole world, including gods and demons, obedient to the command of thy bow, which has lotus fibers for a bowstring and tender flowers in place of arrows?

"Thy friend, O Spring, once gone, will never come back again, as the light of a lamp which the wind has blown out can never come back to it. I am like its wick. See how I am covered with the smoke of sorrow, which chokes me so I cannot stand it any longer.

[31]   "Has not Fate committed a half-murder here? It did not send me to death with Kama. The creeper clings to the sturdy supporting tree, but it falls down when this has been shattered by an elephant.

"Therefore do thou perform for me this duty of friendship without loss of time. Let me die the fiery death in the fullness of my grief and so rest with my husband.

"The moonlight sets along with the moon. The lightning ceases along with the storm. Thus women also go the way of their husbands. Even an inanimate creature recognizes this.

"When I have strewn my bosom with the lovely ashes which are all that is left to me of my beloved's body, I will put myself to sleep on the fire as if on a bed of fresh flowers.

"Good friend, who so often couldst enjoy one bed of flower buds with us, now quickly erect the pyre for me, who have turned to thee as a suppliant, falling at thy feet and joining my hands.

"Then, when thou hast laid the fire on my body, let the

south wind blow and make it blaze up more quickly. Thou knowest very well that Kama will not find a moment's peace without me.

"When thou hast completed this rite, then thou shalt consecrate to us a single handful of water as an offering to the dead. Without dividing it, thy dear friend will drink it with me in the place of departed spirits.

"O Spring, when thou bringest the gifts for the dead, offer to Kama some wind-tossed sprigs of mango flowers. Thy friend loves the mango tree's young shoot."

As Rati thus gave voice to her lament and resolved on death, a voice out of the air consoled her, as the first rain consoles the carp, when it faints in distress because the hot season has dried up the water of the pond.

"O wife of the archer whose arrows are flowers, thy Lord will soon be with thee again. Learn now the reason why he was destroyed like a moth in the fire of Siva's eye.

"Once upon a time the Creator, his passion aroused by Kama, was tempted to enjoy illicit love with his own daughter. He restrained his passion, however, and cursed Kama, and this is the fulfillment of the curse.   [41]

"But when Parvati's asceticism has turned Siva's inclination toward her and he takes her as his bride, then in his joy he will give back to Kama his original body.

"These words, putting an end to the curse on Kama, were pronounced by Brahma at the prayer of Dharma.[30] Indeed, the Self-Controlled One, like a cloud, is now a source of lightning, now a source of nectar.

"Therefore, fair one, keep thy body alive. It will soon be joined to its darling again, for after the rainstorm the river is soon reunited with its water, even though the fiery sun has dried it up."

Thus did an invisible being bring to naught Rati's

resolution to seek her death. Kama's friend placed his faith in it and consoled her with words which conveyed rich meaning in well turned phrases.

And now the love-god's wife, her body worn with grief, waited for the end of her desolation, as the crescent moon, which looks grayish during the daytime because its own light is obscured, yearns for the coming of night.

Canto 5
The Ordeal

When Siva had burned up the god of love in Parvati's presence and so defeated her desire, she spoke in her heart words of reproach against her lovely body, for the only purpose of physical beauty is to please one's beloved.

"When I have completed the labor of ascetic devotion, the charm of my body will no longer be vain" — that was her resolution. In what other way indeed could such love and such a husband be won?

Her heart and soul cleaved only to Siva. But hardly had her mother Mena heard of her daughter's intention to devote herself to ascetic exercises when she took Uma in her arms, discouraged her from the great vow of the ascetics, and spoke to her as follows.

"Thou hast at home the divinities to propitiate. Is such a body as thine, sweetheart, formed for asceticism? The tender acacia flower easily bears the weight of a bee which alights upon it, but not that of a bird."

With such words the mother pleaded with her daughter, but she could not turn the firmly resolved maiden from her purpose. Who can check the mind which hastens toward its desired goal? Who holds back the water plunging into the abyss?

Parvati, true to her vow, sent a close friend to request her father, who knew her desire, that he would permit her to take up her dwelling in the forest, where she might sink her soul in ascetic devotion, destined ultimately to bear fruit.

And when her venerable father, pleased with her determination, which suited her well, had given his consent, Gauri betook herself to the peacock-covered mountain which later became well known among the people of the country by her name.[31]

Firmly resolved, she set aside her pearl necklace, which used to rub off the sandalwood powder on her breasts as it swung back and forth, and put on a garment of birchbark, which shone as ruddy as the early morning sunshine, but which was burst apart by her swelling breasts when it was laced up.

Her face, which had looked beautiful with its hair richly ornamented, was still lovely with its austere braids. The lotus is resplendent with its swarm of bees, yet it is also brilliant when it is mingled with weeds.

When, true to her vow, she first wound round her waist the band she made herself of sedge, triply woven, the place where her waistband had formerly rested became very red.

[11]   Her fingers no longer touched her lips, now left unpainted, but they were cut by the blades of kusha grass she picked. Her hand no longer held her ball, bright with the orange powder of her breasts, but held a rosary instead.

She found her repose on the bare ground, making pillows of her creeper-like arms, she who formerly used to toss back and forth on her rich divan and was tormented even by the flowers dropping from her hair.

Constant in her resolution, she turned over two things to two bystanders as deposits to be taken back later: to the tender creepers her coquettish motions, and to the gazelles her wandering glances.

Untiringly she nourished the young trees with the liquid

issue of the breast-like water jars. Even the war-god will not deprive them of the tenderness which a mother devotes to her sons, for they also were her firstborn.

She gave many a handful of wild corn to the fawns, who got so much confidence in her that she used to match her own eyes against theirs curiously, in the presence of her two companions.

She performed the holy ablutions, made offerings to the fire, wore a tunic of birchbark, and read the sacred scriptures. The seers, however, came hurrying to observe her, for among those who have grown up in religion no consideration is made of age.

This hermitage became so completely sanctified that noxious beasts no longer cherished their former enmity for each other, every guest was greeted with offerings of fruits, and the fire blazed up in the leafy arbor.

When she did not attain the goal she was striving for by her first ascetic exercises, she began to devote herself to even more strenuous asceticism, taking no consideration for her delicate body.

The maiden who had formerly got fatigued by playing with her ball now gave herself up to severe asceticism. Surely her body was made of a golden lotus blossom, by nature both hard and soft at the same time.

The maid, slim-waisted and serene, surrounded herself by four fires, in the summer. She overcame their brilliance, dazzling to the eyes, and then gazed only upon the sun-god, and never in any other direction.

Thus burned by his rays, her face attained the beauty of a lotus blossom, only in the corners of her elongated eyes the blackness gradually left its trace. *[21]*

Her only nourishment was water, which she received without asking, and the rays which the nectareous moon poured down upon her. She lived at that time just like a tree.

Heated by various fires, by that which moves in the sky and by that which is kindled from wood, at the end of the summer, soaked by a sudden shower, she, along with the ground, gave out steam.

The first raindrops found a moment's rest on her eyelashes, touched her lips, splashed as they fell upon her high-arched breast, lingered a little in the folds of her body, and finally came to rest in her deep navel.[32]

As she rested on a rocky ledge without shelter during continuous rainstorms, the nights looked down upon her with their lightning glances, as if they had been made witnesses of her great asceticism.

She spent the nights of winter by the flooded stream, while the winds forever whirled eddies of snow around, but she only felt pity for the ducks there, calling to each other in their separation.[33]

At night her face, which gave out a lotus-like fragrance and shone brightly with its petals of lips, trembling with cold, furnished the stream, as it were, with another lotus blossom to take the place of all the padma blossoms which the snow had killed.

The ultimate degree of asceticism is supposed to be living on the leaves which fall from the tree to the ground of their own accord, but Parvati rejected even these. For this reason the students of the ancient scriptures, to whom she always spoke kindly, gave her the name of Leafless.

By such ascetic practices and others besides, she made her body, tender as a lotus root, waste away day and night. Thus she far surpassed the asceticism which ordinarily only a sturdy hermit can endure.

One day a man entered this grove, carrying a staff of wingseed wood and clad in the hide of a black antelope. He spoke boldly, shone with Brahmanical effulgence, and had braids of hair on his head, so that he appeared to be an incarnation of the first period of life.[34]

Parvati, mindful of hospitality, advanced to greet him
with the honor which respect prescribed. Even where equa-
nimity prevails, those who have overcome their passions behave
with the most delicate consideration for anyone who appears
particularly venerable.

When he had accepted the customary offering which she
presented to him and had in a moment entirely forgotten his
fatigue, he looked Uma in the face and began to address her
according to the rules of etiquette, as follows:

"Hast thou enough tinder and kusha grass for the sacred
rites? Is sufficient water available for the sacred ablutions? Art
thou not lacking in strength for asceticism? The first requisite
of the holy duties is a suitable body.

"Is this young creeper thriving, nourished by water
poured out by thee? It looks like thy lip, which has long been
deprived of red lac, but has remained red none the less.

"Does thy soul remain serene when the tame gazelles take
grass out of thy hand, the gazelles whose roving glances are like
to thy eyes, thou lotus-eyed damsel?

"They say indeed, Parvati, that beauty does not go with
wickedness. This saying now remains true of thy large eyes, for
thy manner of life is a model even for the hermits.

"The waters of the Ganges, plunging down from heaven
and shining with the gifts which are scattered by the Seven
Wise Seers, do not sanctify the mountain king and his race so
much as does the purity of thy deeds.

"Virtue, which is considered the highest of the three goals
of life,[35] seems to me today even more resplendent, noble
maiden, because thou hast attained it and art cultivating it, and
hast freed thy soul from that which is prized as pleasant or
profitable.

"Thou hast paid me unusual honor. Therefore do not
consider me as a stranger, O maiden of graceful form. 'Good
people become friends after seven words' — so say the wise.

"Therefore, thou treasure house of asceticism, who hast

already been very patient, I want to ask thee a question, for my regeneration has made me curious. Give me an answer, then, unless thou art keeping it secret.

[41]   "Birth in the race of the primeval Creator, this body which incarnates the beauty of the three worlds, prosperity in the highest degree so that nothing more need be sought, and youth — tell me, is something better to be expected as a fruit of asceticism?

"We do find such behavior in intelligent women when they are overcome by some intolerable misfortune. But when my mind pursues its course of thought, it does not find this to be thy case, careworn as thou art.

"Thy body knows no distress. How could any mischance happen to thee in thy father's house, maiden of lovely eyebrows? Did a stranger offer thee violence? Is there a man who would reach out his hand to pluck the gem from a serpent's hood?

"Why hast thou put off thy ornaments, wearing already, when still a girl, the birchbark garments which seem beautiful in old age? Does the night, pray, when darkness comes and stars and moon are shining, think of adorning itself with the chariot of the sun?

"If thou art striving for heaven, then thy pains are needless, for thy father's estate is thy heavenly kingdom. But if thou art yearning for a husband, away with this devotion! The pearl does not seek; it is sought.

"I perceive by thy hot sighs that thou art longing for a wooer. Yet my heart is plunged in doubt. I see no man whom thou couldst desire. But if thou dost have such a wish, it would not be difficult to fulfill it.

"That youth, alas, for whom thou hast a longing must be hardhearted indeed, that he does not see the braids upon thy head, shining ruddy as the points of paddy stalks and hanging limply over thy cheeks, which now for a long time have not felt the touch of water lilies on thy ears.

"Say, what rational man's heart would not be grieved at seeing thee visibly wasting away through thy ascetic vow like the waning moon and thy body burned by the sun in all the places where thy ornaments were formerly hung?

"I fear that thy lover is cheated by pride in his beauty, since for a long time he has not made his face an object for thy eyes, which gaze so sweetly with the splendor of their curving lashes.

"How long, Gauri, art thou wearing thyself out? I also performed ascetic exercises in the first period of my life. Accept the half of my asceticism and with it the husband of thy choice. I would learn to know him well."[36]

Thus was the maiden addressed by the brahmin, who [51] penetrated her soul, but the one who had his dwelling in her heart she could not name for shame. She looked only at her female companion, who was standing beside her, while her unpainted eyes kept moving here and there.

The companion, however, spoke to him. "Hear, good sir, if thou hast a desire therefor, why her body is serving as an instrument of asceticism, like a lotus used for shade in the blazing sun.

"The proud maiden has scorned all lords of the four quarters of heaven, Indra and the others, supremely worthy though they be,[37] and wants God the Archer for her husband. But beauty no longer charms him, for Kama is annihilated.

"Although the bearer of the flowery bow was burned to death, the arrow, not reaching Siva with its point, was turned back by his intolerable fury, struck her, and buried itself deep in her heart.

"From that time forth she was feverish with lovesickness in her father's house, her locks discolored by sandalwood powder on her forehead, and not even on rocks made of solid ice could the maid find any rest.

"When the Archer's deeds were sung in ballads, the words would stick in her throat, and her tears would fall, so that the satyr princesses, with whom she used to sing in the forest, would often weep for her.

"And when the third hour of the night came, in which she had closed her eyes for a moment, she would wake up again suddenly. But no one would hear her words, 'Where art thou going, Black Neck?' She would throw her arms around his neck — but it was all a dream and an illusion.

" 'If thou art called omnipresent by the wise, why is the state of my love still unknown to thee?' With such words she would secretly reproach Siva in her frenzy, the Siva which she had painted with her own hands.

"She tried to draw near to the Lord of the World, but no other way was found. So the maiden came to the hermitage with us and her father's consent, in order to practice asceticism here.

"Of the trees here, which owe their whole life to her and which are witnesses of her asceticism, she has seen the fruits, but of her desire to become one with Siva she has never seen a single little shoot.

/61/　　　"We her companions cannot look upon her without tears, for she has wasted completely away through her abstinence. I do not know when he who is easy to seek but hard to find will free our friend from her sorrow, as Indra freed the furrow of the field from its distress when it was in despair for lack of rain."

When the brahmin, who had observed continence his whole life but was still a handsome man, had been told this by the friend who knew the secrets of her heart, so that the true situation became evident, he did not show any sign of joy, but asked Uma, "Is it really so, or is this only a joke?"

The daughter of the mountain, however, who was holding her rosary of rock crystals in her right hand, with the fingers tightly clenched, and who had been standing there silently for some time, was now hardly able to utter the few words which she found.

"As thou, best of all Veda scholars, hast heard, I am striving for a high place. My asceticism is only a means to reach it. These wishes of mine do not seem to be hopeless."

To this the brahmin answered as follows: "I know God Siva well. Thou art attracted to him. But when I consider that he delights in frightful habits, I cannot give thee my approval in this matter.

"My girl, thou art stubbornly pursuing vain things. How indeed can thy hand, when the marriage cord is bound around it, endure the very first touch of Siva's hand, with its bracelet of serpents?

"Consider this thyself: Are these two things ever fit to be joined together, a young girl's satin gown embroidered with swans and his elephant hide dripping drops of blood?

"Tell me, would thy worst enemy consent to have thy feet, which were covered by masses of flowers in the great hall, leave their prints and their traces of red dye in the cemetery, where the hairs of corpses are strewn around?

"Say whether there is anything more incongruous than this, assuming it could occur, than that thou shouldst embrace Siva, covering thy bosom with the dust of funeral pyre ashes instead of its accustomed yellow sandalwood powder.

"Moreover, it will be a source of ridicule for thee when the people see thee, as a bride, riding on an old bull, although worthy to be borne by a king of elephants, and they stand around laughing.

"Because of thy desire to be joined with Siva there are *[71]* now two things to be pitied: the crescent moon shining in beauty on Siva's head, and that which shines with equal beauty, thyself, moonlight for the eyes of the world.

"His beauty is a misplaced eye, the God's lineage cannot be traced, his wealth can be known by the fact that the sky is his only covering. O damsel, whose eyes are like those of a fawn, can a single one of those properties which are ordinarily sought in wooers be found in Siva?

"Turn thy mind away from this evil desire. What a chasm yawns between him, who is thus constituted, and thee, who hast all beautiful properties! A good man does not want a sacred sacrifice, performed with recitation of Vedas at the sacrificial stake, to be undertaken at such a stake as is set up in a cemetery."

When the brahmin had spoken these unkindly words, her anger showed itself by the quivering of her lips. She looked to the side with her eyes, their corners gleaming red, and her eyebrows were contracted.

Then she answered him. "Since thou speakest like that to me, thou dost not know Siva in reality. Foolish persons always hate the doings of highminded ones, which are strange, and the motives for which are incomprehensible to them.

"A man turns to such things, which are said to bring happiness, if he wants to escape from some misfortune, or if he puts happiness in the possession of wealth. But Siva, who is indifferent and who shelters the universe — what has he to do with all this, which only torments the heart with cravings?

"Although poor, he is the source of all riches. He who wanders around in cemeteries is considered Lord of the three worlds. And he, who is always called frightful, is named Gracious. I know of none who knows him as he really is.

"He may be resplendent with jewels or wear serpents, he may be clad in the elephant hide or in a silken gown, he may go around with skulls or be radiant with glittering moonlight — the body of him whose form is the universe can never be determined.

"Surely the ashes of the funeral pyre become perfectly pure when they come in contact with his body. When he bows down in his pantomimic dance, the diadems of all the gods accompany him, as everybody knows.

"But when Indra, on his celestial elephant sprinkling its love-juice, bows his crowned head low before him, riding on his bull like a poor man, he makes this God's toes brilliant with a reddish glow from the pollen which falls from the full blown flowers of the coral-tree.

"That which thou, wicked man, wouldst reckon as a fault, [81] was said all too truly. How can the lineage be traced of him who is called the source of Brahma?

"Enough of argument between us! Let him be just as thou hast said. My heart feels itself drawn to him in pure love. A lover does not listen to words of abuse.

"My friend, send this fellow away. His lips are trembling. He will speak again. Not only he who speaks evil of a great person but also he who merely hears the slander spoken, is guilty of sin at that very moment."

And with the words, "Or shall I go away from here?" the maid was hurrying away, her birchbark garment burst open by her breasts, but Siva, assuming his own form, drew her to him with a smile.

Scarcely did she behold the God when she began to tremble, broke out in perspiration all over her slender body, and held suspended the foot she had already raised. Thus the mountain princess neither went nor stood. She was like a river which becomes turbulent when a rock obstructs its current.

And now Siva spoke to her, "From today forth, O maiden of delicate body, I am thy slave, bought by thy asceticism." Immediately all her fatigue, arising from her sacred labors, was forgotten. Toil produces new spirit when its fruit is finally obtained.

Canto 6
The Betrothal

Soon after this, Gauri secretly sent her companion to the God whose body is the universe with the message, "The monarch of all mountains gives me in marriage. Thou must consult him."

When the confidante delivered her message, the mountain's daughter appeared with her in her beloved's presence without speaking, like the mango bud with the singing cuckoo when spring is near.

Saying, "So be it," Siva assented, took leave of Uma reluctantly, and then called to mind the Seven Wise Seers made of light.

They, rich in asceticism, immediately appeared before Siva's face, together with Arundhati.[38] Their shining halos filled the air with light.

They had bathed in the celestial Ganges, where sweet fragrance arises from the love-juice of the elephants which stand as guardians of the four quarters of heaven, and where the waves toss up the blossoms of the coral trees growing on its banks.

Their sacrificial cords were strings of pearls. They wore birchbark garments embroidered with gold. Their rosaries were made of precious stones. Thus they were like wishing-trees devoted to the wandering life.

The sun-god, driving his steeds and waving his banner far below, bowed before them, for even he looked up to them.

Even at the terrible time of universal dissolution they remained serenely on the Boar's[39] great tusk, together with the earth, which was uprooted by him and clung to their creeper-like arms.

After Brahma they created the rest of the world. Therefore the wise men of old gave them the name of "the Ancient Creators."

Although they were enjoying the pure and fully ripened fruits of past asceticisms, nevertheless they still remained ascetics.

The chaste seeress Arundhati, looking down at her /11/ husband's feet, shone in their midst like the reward of asceticism incarnate.

Siva looked upon her and all the hermits with equal respect. Men and women should be considered equal, for good character is all that counts.

When he saw Arundhati, his desire to take a wife grew even greater. Virtuous, noble women are surely the primary inspiration for righteous undertakings.

And because Siva was also moved by duty to take Parvati as his wife, Kama's spirit, fearful because of the defeat it had suffered before, was filled with new hope.

All the hermits did reverence to Siva. Those sages, deeply learned in the Vedas and Vedangas, spoke as follows, while their body hairs stirred with ecstasy:

"If we have duly studied the Brahmanas, sacrificed to the fire-god according to the prescribed ritual, and accomplished works of asceticism, we now reap the full reward of all this at once.

"For through thee, the Lord of the world, we have achieved a place in thy mind, which formerly surpassed our fondest hopes.

"He in whose mind thou establishest thy dwelling is the

foremost of the wise, but much more even is he to be considered wise who dwells in thy mind, the source of Brahma.

"True it is we occupy a place which towers higher than the moon's, loftier than the sun's. But through thy grace in thinking of us we, who surpass these two, have today attained such a state.

"Being thus honored by thee, we now value ourselves highly. Confidence in our own qualities is naturally aroused by the esteem of superiors.

[21]   "But can we possibly make the bliss which thy thinking of us has produced any better known to thee, Siva? Thy mind penetrates into all mankind.

"Thou standest before our eyes, but we do not yet know thee fully. Be gracious unto us. Reveal thyself to us. Thou dwellest not upon the ways which thoughts pursue.

"Is this that part of thyself by which thou createst the visible world? Or is it that by which thou preservest it? Or that by which thou finally bringest the whole universe to destruction?

"But this great question may better remain unasked. Rather command us what we shall do for thee, we who, barely thought of, already stand in thy presence."

And now the Supreme Lord answered the seers, while the bright flashes of his teeth added to the soft light of the moon shining on his brow.

"You know well that I never act from self-seeking. Have I not, in my eight forms, shown myself to the world to be entirely free from self-devotion?

"But all the gods, who are oppressed by enemies, are beseeching me, though free from self-seeking, nevertheless to beget a son, as cuckoos tormented by thirst supplicate the cloud to send them rain at last.

"Therefore I will take Parvati to wife in order to beget a son, as the sacrificer takes the rubbing-stick in order to kindle the fire.[40]

"You are to sue Himalaya for her in my name. Alliances mediated by virtuous persons always turn out successfully.

"You must know that I am not humbled by uniting myself in marriage with him who is lofty and sturdy and bears the weight of the world.

"I do not need to instruct you with what words to speak to him about his daughter, for you are yourselves the exemplars from whom wise persons take their rules of conduct.

[31]

"The venerable lady Arundhati shall be our assistant in this, for the skill of respectable ladies is usually desirable in such affairs.

"Do you, then, proceed to Oshadhiprastha, the snowy mountain's city, to accomplish this affair. Then we will all assemble again at the Mahakoschi cataract."

When all the ascetics, sons of the Creator, now saw that he himself, the Prince of all hermits, intended to celebrate his marriage, they no longer felt any shame for having themselves once taken wives.

The group of seers uttered the word "Aum" and set out upon their journey. Siva, however, went to the place he had designated.

The mighty seers flew up to the sky, shining somber like a sword, and came to Oshadhiprastha with the speed of thought.

This city lay there as if Alaka, home of the god of wealth, had been transplanted there and filled with all the treasures of the celestial world.

It was surrounded by the stream of the Ganges, herbs glittered on its ramparts, its walls were built of great blocks of precious stone. Even in its fortifications it was charming to the heart.

There the elephants lived free from the fear of lions. Its horses were of the stock of Indra's stud, its citizens were elves and goblins, its women were nymphs.

Clouds cling to the gables of its houses, in which the

beating of drums is confused with the reverberations of thunder and distinguished only by the rhythm.

[41]   Garments hanging on the wishing-trees and fluttering in the wind provide the gay banners which appear in other cities on the flagpoles of houses, without any care on the part of the citizens.

In the crystal palaces, which possess many drinking halls, the reflection of the stars provides the gifts which elsewhere would be flowers or jewels.

At night, in rainy weather, darkness is something quite unknown to lovelorn damsels, for the bright phosphorescence of the herbs shows them the way which they wish to go.

There a lifetime always ends with the restoration of youth. There is no other slayer than the god of love. There is no loss of consciousness except the sleep which follows the fatigue of making love.

When its women are angry, their arched eyebrows, quivering lips, and threatening fingers are lovely, and make their lovers entreat them until they gain their favor.

Its pleasure resort is Mount Gandhamadana, where a pleasant fragrance fills the air and vagabond elves sleep in the shade of the champak.

When the divine sages saw Mount Himalaya's city lying thus, they felt that doing good deeds for gaining heaven is only an illusion.

While the gatekeepers, looking up, recognized them by their heavy braids like painted firebrands, they descended in great haste to the mountain monarch's palace.

Coming down from the sky and following each other in order of age, the group of anchorites shone like a row of suns reflected in a stream of water.

When the seers were still at some distance, however, the mountain came forth to meet them with guest offerings, bowing the earth under his heavy steps.

[51]   Bloodstone formed his ruddy lips. He towered high.

Fragrant pine trees were his sturdy arms. Nature had formed his breast of a great rocky cliff. It was quite obviously Himalaya.

He respectfully welcomed the immaculately virtuous sages with due ceremony, showed them the way personally, and escorted them into the inmost apartment of his palace.

There he took his place, joined his hands reverently, and spoke these words to the seers, who were seated on cane stools.

"Like a rain which falls without any gathering of clouds and like a fruit of which no flower has been seen, thus unexpected does your appearance here seem to me.

"By this mark of your favor I am like a fool who has suddenly become a wise man, iron which is transmuted into gold, and one who has risen from this world to heaven.

"From today forth I can serve all beings as a means of sanctification. A place which holy personages have visited is considered a shrine.

"I feel myself purified by two things, by the cataract of the Ganges falling on my head, and by the waters which have washed your feet, you regenerate ones.

"Through your favor I see my body honored in both its forms. The personified and movable is waiting at your service; the immovable bears the impression of your feet.

"Although my limbs extend to the confines of the quarters of heaven, yet they cannot contain the ever increasing joy arising from this token of your condescension.

"Through my seeing you and your brightness, not only the darkness of my caves is dispelled, but also the spiritual darkness resulting from passions.

"I can imagine nothing which I could do for you *[61]* here – though if anything were found, what would be impossible? I believe that you have come to me only in order to sanctify my soul.

"Nevertheless you should now give me your command for some service, for commissions from their lords are only favors for the servants.

"Here I offer you myself, here is my wife, here also my daughter, the life of the family. Only say how I can be of service to you. I make no mention of material things."

Thus spoke Himalaya to the seers, repeating his words, as it were, by the echoes resounding from the mouths of his caves.

They, however, urged Angirasa, who was always the first when it came to speaking, to make a reply, which he phrased in the following words.

"All that thou hast said is true of thee, and also much besides. Thy soul and thy summit are equally lofty.

"Rightly art thou called God Vishnu in the garb of stability. Thy bosom has become the refuge for all nature, animate and inanimate.

"How could the Serpent hold up the earth with its lotus-like hood, if thou didst not support thyself upon the foundations of the underworld?

"Thy glory and thy rivers, in solid clear rows not bound by the waves of the sea, sanctify the whole world.

"If the Ganges acquires renown from Vishnu's foot,[41] it acquires it likewise from its second source, namely from thee, towering aloft.

[71]   "When Vishnu took his three paces,[42] his greatness was extended in all directions, into the heights and depths. But thou includest all this within thyself.

"The golden summit of Mount Meru is as nothing, for thou hast attained a place in the pantheon of the gods.

"Thou hast assigned thy inflexibility to thy immovable body, but thy personified form is inclined to deference and ever seeks to be of service to the good.

"Therefore learn now the reason for our coming. It concerns only thee, yet we, as bearers of the tidings to thee, have a partial interest in it also.

"He who bears the crescent moon upon his brow, together with the mighty title 'Lord,' which is not given to others; who has the power to make himself as tiny as an atom, and other powers as well;

"Who bears the universe by means of his eight forms, earth and the others, mutually strengthening each other like horses drawing a chariot on the road;

"Who is sought by all yogis; who dwells in all bodies; who is subject to no fear of rebirth — so the wise tell us;

"He, Siva, the Dispenser of desired boons and the Contemplator of every act of the All, sues for thy daughter by these words entrusted to us.

"Thou shalt unite him with her as one unites the correct meaning with the word. A father does not consider his daughter to be lamented when she obtains a good man as her husband.

"As many beings as may exist, inanimate and animate, all will consider her as their Mother, for Siva is the Father of the world.

"When the gods kneel before the dark-necked God, then [81] they will endue her feet with a bright radiance from the brilliant jewels shining on their heads.

"Uma is the bride. Thou art he who gives her away. We are the petitioners. God Siva is the suitor. It suffices for the beatitude of thy race.

"By the union of thy daughter with him thou shalt become the father of the God who is called Father of the universe, who himself raises hymns to none but receives hymns offered to him, who himself does homage to none but to whom homage is done."

While the divine seer was thus speaking, Parvati was standing at her father's side, looking down, and counting off the petals of the lotus blossom which she carried as a plaything.

Although the mountain was filled with the desire to give his daughter away, he first looked at Mena's face. In matters concerning daughters the heads of families usually follow the views of their wives.

But Mena realized that she must accord with her husband's desire, for devoted wives never oppose that which their husbands wish to do.

"I will say this as a proper answer" — thus he was considering in his mind; and at the end of the seer's speech he took his daughter, who was standing beside him in her auspicious ornaments, by the hand.

"Come, sweetheart, thou art chosen as an offering to Siva. These hermits here are asking for it. Now the fruit of my married life is fully ripened!"

The mountain spoke only these words to his daughter, but to the company of seers he said, "The wife of the three-eyed God bows here before you all."

The sages gave their approval to what the mountain said, for his fair words indeed fulfilled their wish, and then pronounced a blessing on Uma, with wishes which were soon to be realized.

[91]   The blushing bride bowed down so low that her golden earrings touched the ground, but Arundhati took her on her lap.

She then comforted Uma's mother, who was grief-stricken and weeping because of her great love for her daughter, by describing to her the virtues of the bridegroom, who would not marry any other wife.

When the bark-clad seers were now asked by Siva's future relatives what would be a favorable day of the moon for the wedding, they answered, "It shall be three days from today." Then they all hastened away again.

They bade farewell to Himalaya, sought out Siva again, informed him that they had fulfilled their mission, were thereupon dismissed by him, and ascended from the earth up to the sky again.

Siva, however, could hardly wait these few days. He was longing to be joined at once to the mountain princess. If such feelings disturb even the Lord, what a turmoil they must arouse in an ordinary person, who has not yet obtained mastery over himself!

Canto 7
The Wedding

As the lord of herbs grew full, and the day of the month arrived on which Libra displayed its favoring presence, Himalaya, together with all the relatives of his family, celebrated the solemnization of matrimony for his daughter.

All the housewives, in every home, enraptured with joy and delight, were busy with their preparations. Thus it seemed as if the whole city formed a single household with the people of the harem.

The boulevards of the capital were thickly strewn with champak blossoms, many banners woven of Chinese silk fluttered in the breeze, the golden gates were radiant, and the whole city shone as if paradise had been transported to that place.

Although her parents had many children, Uma became their whole life, now that they realized that her marriage was about to take place. It was as if they had not seen her for a long time, or as if she had risen from the dead.

She made her way from bosom to bosom, amid the blessings of all, and received one piece of jewelry after another. Although the affection of the mountain monarch's family was divided among many relatives, it was now all concentrated on this one maiden.

At the hour which is sacred to god Mitra, the twelfth lunar house being in conjunction with the moon, those of her female relatives who had husbands and children began to make her toilet.

She was attired in a satin garment reaching above the navel, such as women and girls were accustomed to wear while anointing the body. Its sheen was now increased by the ointment of durva grass mixed with white mustard.

Touching a new arrow, as the marriage ritual required, the maiden now shone like the crescent moon when it is illumined by the rays of the sun after the close of the dark fortnight.

When her body oil had been absorbed by lodhra paste, she was sprinkled with powder of dry black sandalwood, attired in a bathrobe, and conducted to the square, four-columned bathing hall.

In this hall, resplendent with pearl decorations and embellished with emerald inlays, the women bathed her with streams of water which they poured over her from eight-footed urns, amid the sound of music.

[11]   When her body had been purified by this auspicious bath, she put on a garment suitable for greeting the bridegroom with all honor. Thus she shone like the earth when it covers itself with kusha grass after a rain.

Surrounded by chaste matrons, she was now led from there to the place of the nuptial altar, which was supported on four columns of precious stone and furnished with a seat and cushion.

Having seated the slender maiden there, with her face looking toward the east, they paused a little while, sitting before her, although many articles of adornment were lying ready at hand, for their eyes were charmed by the natural beauty of her body.

Her luxuriant hair was strewn with flowers and dried with perfumed air, and one of the women plaited it into a splendid braid with a garland of white illupi flowers interwoven with durva grass.

Then they adorned her with white sandalwood powder and painted streaks on her with a saffron salve. Thus she stood there surpassing in beauty the three-coursed Ganges with yellow ducks sitting on its sandy banks.

Her beautiful countenance with her splendidly decorated locks outshone the lotus blossom with its swarm of bees and even the orb of the moon with its wisps of clouds, and abolished their use as standards of comparison.

And above all the lovely barley stalk adorning her ear drew the charmed eyes of all who looked upon her to her cheek, which was covered with lodhra paste and radiant with saffron rouge.

Her lips were like a ripe fruit, their contour defined by a line, their redness emphasized a little by beeswax. Their quivering increased the ineffable beauty of this maiden, symmetrical in every part.

Her friend, who was dyeing her feet, gave her this blessing in jest, "Touch with this foot the crescent on thy husband's head." Uma struck her with her garland, but said not a word in reply.

But the women who were attiring her looked at her eyes, which glowed as lovely as the beautiful petals of a lotus blossom, and painted them with black paint, not in the hope of making them even more beautiful, but only because they believed that this would bring her good fortune.

Adorned now with all her ornaments, she was as [21] resplendent as a creeper with its full blown blossoms, as the night with its shining stars, as a river with birds sitting on it.

Radiant, she looked at herself in the mirror with big, fixed eyes, and thought only of Siva's coming, for the adornment of women has for its purpose to be seen by the beloved.

And now her mother took the auspicious moist yellow paint mixed with red arsenic on two fingers, and lifted the face of Uma, from whose ears white pendants of carved ivory hung down.

She was scarcely able to mark the nuptial tilaka on her daughter's brow. This was what had ever been the desire of her heart, a desire which had been growing along with Uma's breasts.

Her eyes were so blinded by tears that she bound the woolen nuptial cord on her daughter's wrist in a wrong way, but her nurse then wound it in the right place.

Uma's body was clothed in new satin, and her hand grasped the new mirror, so that she now shone as brilliantly as the shore of the ocean covered with foam or as an autumn night with a full moon.

To her, who was to perpetuate the family, her mother said, "Venerate the venerable gods of thy family." After that, knowing what ceremonies were necessary, she had her daughter bow low before each of the chaste matrons.

Uma bowed down and received their parting wishes, "Mayst thou enjoy thy husband's undivided love." But actually Parvati went far beyond this blessing of her relatives, for she became one flesh with Siva.[43]

Having thus fulfilled his duties for his daughter in a way which accorded with his wish and with his wealth, the happy mountain, accustomed as he was to fine manners, took his place with his friends in his assembly hall, to wait there for Siva's arrival.

And for him, meanwhile, on Kuvera's mountain, the Mothers were busy in laying out adornment suitable for his first marriage.

[31]   These beautiful and auspicious ornaments were merely touched by the Lord, out of regard for the women. The God's own attire underwent a transformation which made it seemly for a bridegroom.

His ashes became white powder, his skull assumed the splendor of a bright diadem, and instead of his elephant hide there appeared a gold-embroidered robe.

The third eye which gleamed on his brow with its reddish brown pupil took the place of the tilaka which is made of yellow paint.

The bodies of the princely cobras twined about his limbs were transformed into the most beautiful ornaments, but the radiance of their crest gems remained unchanged.

What need had Siva of a crown? His eternal diadem is the moon, shining even by day. The eye cannot perceive its dark spot, for it is only a crescent.

When thus he had produced this beautiful costume by his own power and as sole cause of the miracle, he looked at his reflection in a sword, brought to him by his hosts, who were near at hand.

Then, leaning on Nandi's arm, he mounted his bull, as if he were climbing Mount Kailasa. The back of this animal was covered with a tiger skin. He contracted the huge extent of his body out of veneration for his master, and they set forth.

All the Mothers followed the God, their earrings swinging back and forth with the motion of their vehicles,[44] their halos shining red like the lotus blossom's pollen. Their countenances transformed the sky, as it were, into a pond in which lotus blossoms are blooming.

They glittered like gold, and behind them the Black Goddess,[45] with her garland of skulls, shone like a range of thunderclouds surrounded by flocks of fluttering cranes and shooting forth flashes of lightning before itself.

That the favorable time had now come for all the gods to do their homage to Siva was announced by the auspicious sound of his own hosts' instruments resounding in the horns of the celestial chariots.

Over him the sun-god held a new umbrella from the [41] workshop of the celestial craftsman Twashtri. Siva's diadem shone close against its fabric, so that it seemed as if the cataract of the Ganges were falling on his head.

Ganges and Jumna, incarnate, attended him with fly-brushes.[46] Although both had set aside the functions of rivers, they could still be recognized as if by their fluttering swans.

The primeval Creator approached him in visible form, and also Vishnu, his breast adorned with the Srivatsa. Both magnified his glory with the word, "Victory!" as one augments the flame with a sacrifice.

His single substance was divided into three, but each of these three persons might appear both as first and as last. Thus Siva would precede God Vishnu, Vishnu would precede him, Brahma would precede them both, or again both Vishnu and Siva would take precedence over Brahma.

The guardians of the world, Indra and the others, now set aside their regalia and all humbly prostrated themselves before Siva with joined hands. Nandi announced each of them correctly, as they made themselves known by gestures, so that Siva was able to recognize them all.

He greeted Brahma with a bow, Vishnu with words, Indra with a smile, each of the other gods merely with a look, as accorded with their various ranks.

The Seven Wise Seers, however, expressed to him the wish, "May thou be victorious!" To this he replied, "You have already been chosen by me as priests for the nuptial sacrifice which we are celebrating here."

And now Vishvavasu and other gifted singers took up their strain, singing of the victories which he won over Tripura long ago, and to this music the bearer of the crescent moon, whom the delusions of spiritual darkness can never overcome, proceeded along his way.

He was borne by his bull, which swayed back and forth as he went through the sky, so that his little golden bells tinkled. He kept shaking his horns, which pierced the clouds and so looked as if they were covered with clay derived from goring the riverbank in sport.

Drawn on by the rays shot from Siva's eyes like threads of gold, he came in the twinkling of an eye to the city of which the mountain monarch is the guardian and which no enemy has ever entered.

The inhabitants of the city, watching the sky full of curiosity, now saw the God approaching them, his neck as dusky as a cloud. He sped along the path marked by his own arrows and descended to the surface of the earth nearby. *[51]*

The mountain prince, rejoicing at his arrival, came forth to meet him, with many elephants on which his relatives, richly clad, were seated, as if with his mountain slopes on which trees, in full bloom, were standing.

At the city gate, which was thrown open, the host of gods united with the host of mountains amid a tumult which could be heard afar, like two rivers coming together with a far sounding roar and breaking through a single floodgate.

When Siva, Lord of the three worlds, bowed to the mountain monarch, the latter felt embarrassed, having quite forgotten that he himself had just made an obeisance before the divine majesty.

His handsome countenance beaming with joy, he preceded his son-in-law and escorted him into his rich city, on the principal streets of which the flowers were strewn profusely, ankle deep.

At this moment the fair ladies of the city appeared in the rows of palaces, dropping all other activities in their eagerness to see the God of gods.

One, suddenly hurrying to the window, was unable to finish binding up her long hair, but held it back with her hand. The garland of flowers had already dropped down from the untied ribbon.

Another snatched her right foot away from her maid,

who was holding it and dyeing it with liquid lac. She forgot her usual coquettish walk, and marked her way to the window with drops of the red lac.

A third, who had made up her right eye but had not yet done the left, rushed to the window with the eyebrow pencil still in her hand.

A fourth did not retie her loincloth, which had become loosened as she ran, but only gazed through the window. Thus she stood there, holding the garment close against her body with her hand, the jewels on which illumined her navel.

[61]   The half wound pearl belt of a fifth woman, who had jumped up hurriedly, which kept slipping farther down at every heedless step, finally remained hanging with its strings against her great toe.

The windows, filled with the faces of the eager women, whose breath was fragrant with wine and whose eyes darted back and forth like bees, were as brilliant as if they had been decorated with lotus blossoms.[47]

Meanwhile Siva was coming onto the royal boulevard, where many flags were flying and the arched gates towered up to heaven. He caused the spires of the palaces to be bathed in moonlight even in the daytime, so that they shone with double beauty.

The women gazed upon the peerless God and drank him in with their eyes, ignoring everything else. All their other senses strove to enter into their eyes, as it were.

"Quite rightly did Leafless endure the severe asceticism for his sake, even though she possesses such a delicate body. One who could merely say, 'I am his slave girl,' would be at the summit of happiness – but how much more so the wife who rests on his bosom."

"If the Creator did not unite this couple, whose charm is the envy of all, then the pains which he has devoted to the creation of beauty would be fruitless."

"Surely the body of the bearer of the flowery bow was not burned up by him in anger. I believe that when Kama saw this God, he gave up his own body for shame."

"The mountain prince, my dear, whose head already rises high because he supports the earth, will hold it still higher when he fulfills his desire, oh how happily! by becoming allied with this Lord."

Such words as these, which sounded sweet in his ears, were heard by Siva, spoken by the fair ladies of the city of Oshadhiprastha, as he approached the residence of Himalaya, near which many handfuls of rice were shattered against many bracelets.[48]

God Vishnu held out his hand to Siva, who dismounted from his bull like the sun-god coming out from a white autumnal cloud, and proceeded into the great hall of the mountain monarch's palace, where Brahma had already entered.

He was followed by Indra and the other gods, the Seven *[71]* Seers, and the great sages, together with the hosts, all hastening to the mountain palace, as a momentous work is accompanied by mighty means.

There the Lord and Master seated himself and accepted all the customary offerings, with due ceremony: first the offering of water, together with precious stones, then curds mixed with honey, finally two new garments, which the mountain prince presented to him.

Thereupon, arrayed in a silken robe, he was conducted by eunuchs skilled in ceremonial to the side of his beloved, as the sea, with its mass of white foam, is drawn by the rays of the newly risen moon to where the shore is.

As he, whose eyes were like full blown lotus blossoms, now united himself with her, resplendent with a radiant countenance like that of the full moon, the torrent of his soul became clear and calm like the world when the beauty of the full moon shines over it in autumn.

At this moment of union the eyes of both were closed in embarrassment. Then, when their eyes happened to meet, they would stay fixed for a moment, gazing at each other passionately, but then, becoming nervous, they would turn away again.

Siva now clasped the maiden's rosy-fingered hand, which the mountain monarch's priest placed in his, as if it were the first little bud of the god of love who seized by fear had hidden himself in Uma's body.

Her body hairs stirred in ecstasy, while the God whose banner bears a bull began to perspire in the fingers. The manifestation of the god of love was conveyed to both in equal measure, as it were, by the joining of their hands.

Any couple display the height of beauty when they join their hands together. How, then, shall I describe the loveliness of these two, as they stood beside each other?

When this couple walked in a circle from right to left around the brightly burning fire, they shone like Day and Night encircling, close together, the border of Mount Meru.

The family priest now led the bride and groom, who closed their eyes as they touched each other, three times around the fire, and then made the young woman throw parched grains of rice into its brightly blazing flame.

[81]   Thereupon, instructed by the priest, she drew to her face a handful of smoke from the burning grains. As the wisps of smoke hovered over her cheeks, they became for an instant like ear pendants of lotus blossoms for the young bride.

As she inhaled the smoke, according to an ancient ritual, her cheeks became moist and ruddy, the color of the black paint in her eyes began to run, and the barley stalk hanging from her ear wilted.

The brahmin, however, addressed her. "My child, this fire here is the witness of thy marriage. Now, with Siva thy bridegroom, fulfill without hesitation the duties which the Law teaches thee."

Uma, stretching her ears open as far as the corners of her eyes, drank in the priest's words, as the earth, glowing with heat at the end of the dry season, drinks in the first rain.

Her beautiful and immortal Bridegroom now bade her to direct her gaze upon the polestar. She did so, but thereupon her head dropped down in embarrassment, her voice stuck in her throat, and she could scarcely utter the words, "I saw it."

Thus the Himalaya's family priest, who knew all the scriptures, brought the solemn ceremony of joining hands to its conclusion. Then the parents of all creation bowed before Brahma, who was sitting on a lotus throne.

The Creator gave the young woman his blessing with the following words: "Mayst thou, fair one, give birth to a hero." But when he tried to think of a blessing for Siva, he was obliged to keep silent, although he is considered the Lord of Eloquence, because Siva is absolutely desireless.

Then they went to the square sacrificial altar, where many articles of finery were displayed. There they sat on golden thrones, and set their feet on unhusked grain, a custom usual and expected among the people.

The Goddess Lakshmi[49] held over them both an umbrella represented by a long stemmed lotus blossom. It shone brilliantly with its lacework of pearls, formed by drops of water clinging to the edge of its petals.

The Goddess Saraswati[50] sang the praise of the couple in a twofold style of language. The renowned bridegroom was lauded in words made clear by correct syntax, but the young wife in a form of speech which she could easily understand.[51]

For a while they watched the performance of the celestial *[91]* nymphs, which displayed a different style in every scene, in which the melodies were adapted to the various emotions represented, and in which the dancing was beautiful.

As soon as it reached its end, all the gods prostrated themselves before the newly married Siva, raising their hands and clasping them upon their crowns. Again they besought him to accept the service of Kama, who at the termination of the curse assumed his own body again.

The mighty God, no longer moved by anger, now allowed Kama to direct his arrows upon him, for the petitions of dutiful servants to their lords and masters are sure to attain their end.

Then Siva dismissed the host of gods, took the mountain princess by the hand, and went with her into the bridal chamber, where golden water jars were standing, bedding was spread on the ground, and many gifts brightened the room.

Gauri, however, blushing with embarrassment, because marriage was new for her, turned her face away again when he drew it to him, and could scarcely speak a word even to her two best friends who used to sleep with her. But Siva made her smile secretly by the funny faces of his goblin attendants.

Canto 8
The Consummation

After the wedding ceremony Parvati was filled with love and apprehension at the same time, so that, when she looked at Siva, her body was a sight to charm his heart, for he was filled with desire.

When he spoke to the Goddess, she would make no answer, but would hold her gown close with her hand and try to go away. When she lay on their bed, she would turn her face away from him. But even by this behavior she only aroused the Bowbearer's love.

She would fix one eye on her beloved when he seemed to be asleep — but he would only be pretending, out of curiosity. Then when he awoke, smiling, she would shut it quick as a flash.

When he laid his hand over the young bride's navel, she would push it back, her body quivering. But the waistband of her garment would become loosened of its own accord.

Her handmaidens had said, "Enjoy the secret pleasures of love with Siva, dear. Don't be afraid." But when she actually saw the idol of her heart before her face, she became so confused that she forgot their counsel.

When her instructor in the art of love kept asking new questions, so that the talk was uninterrupted although often no real meaning could be found in it, she would reply by shaking her head so that her eyes embraced him completely.

When he took off her clothes in the privacy of their chamber, she would cover his eyes with her hands. But the eye on his forehead still shone, so she despaired of this, seeing that her effort was futile.

The pleasure he enjoyed with his young bride, kissing her without biting her lower lip, taking her in his arms tenderly, and resting his hands on her breasts only lightly, was sweet and dear to him, although the god of love was grieved and disappointed by her lack of response.

She would submit only to that sort of love in which he showed himself gentle and tender, in which her lips remained unwounded when he kissed them and her body did not suffer from the scratches of his nails.

In the morning, when her girl friends asked, "What happened during the night?" she would not satisfy their curiosity, for shame. But what her tongue would not betray, her heart would quickly reveal.

[11]   And when she observed in her hand glass how making love had altered her appearance, and also saw in it, beside her own image, that of her beloved, who was standing behind her — what wouldn't she do, overcome by shame!

But when her mother saw that Siva was happily enjoying Uma's youth, she sighed for pure joy. Every woman brings to an end her mother's care when her husband treats her with tenderness.

Nevertheless it was still several days before Siva finally succeeded in bringing it about that Parvati herself had a desire for making love. Gradually, however, her stubbornness toward the pleasure of love disappeared.

When he pressed against her breasts, she would throw her arms around him. When he wanted to kiss her face, she would no longer turn it away. Now she would hold his hand away only lightly when it lustfully grasped the belt wound around her hips.

Their affection revealed itself by many signs. There was never an unloving word, only loving ones. When one of them went away for even a short while, the other was despondent. The tenderness of the bride and groom, which grew greater as time passed, was mutual.

The young wife took delight in the husband so well suited to her, and he turned to her with equally loving devotion. The Ganges, indeed, never flows away from Ocean, and Ocean's greatest joy is the kiss of her mouth.

She secretly gave herself to Siva as a pupil. He instructed her in making love, while for her pupil's fee she paid him with all those lover's crafts into which he had initiated her.

When he bit her lips, her fingers quivered with pain, but at the end of the kiss the pain was immediately cured by the cool rays of the moon on his head.

When the eye on his brow was filled with powder dropping from her tresses, it was soothed again in the stream of her breath, which gave out a sweet fragrance like full blown lotus blossoms.

Proceeding thus along the way of passion, Siva restored Kama to his favor, and spent a month long honeymoon with Uma in the palace of the mountain prince.

Then, bidding farewell to Himalaya, who was stricken *[21]* with grief at parting from his daughter, and mounting his bull, whose swiftness is immeasurable, he roamed at large, on pleasure bent.

Filled with happiness and desire, and held by Uma close to her bosom, he was borne to Mount Meru, riding on this animal, which made the journey with the speed of the wind. There he took his pleasure on beds with inlaid golden tendrils, but all constructed strong enough to stand the stress of love.

Constantly hovering about Uma's lotus face like a bee

seeking honey, he found repose on the slopes of Mount Mandara, covered with cool drops of nectar and Vishnu's bracelets.[52]

Then on Mount Kailasa the Lord of the Three Worlds reveled in the light of the clear moonbeams. But she would throw the fetters of her tender arms around his neck in fright,[53] thinking that the demon prince Ravana might be thundering again.

One time, when he was enjoying lovemaking with Uma among the hills of Malaya, the south wind wafted away their exhaustion like a flatterer, for it had been shaking the sandalwood branches and was laden with filaments from the clove tree.

Another time she struck her beloved with a golden lotus. Then he splashed her with water from his hand, so that she closed her eyes and ducked in the stream, where a circle of fishes made her a second belt.

In the celestial park Nandana he decorated her with parijata blossoms, Sachi's[54] favorite hair ornaments, but the goddesses regarded her with jealousy.

Thus Siva and his bride enjoyed the pleasures of heaven and earth. Finally, one day at the hour when the sun was beginning to turn red, they settled down on the woody slope of Mount Gandhamadana.

There he stretched himself out on a golden rock, with the sun shining brightly before his face, and his wife rested her body on his left arm. Gazing at the setting sun, he spoke to her as follows:

"It seems as if the lord of day has placed the lotus blossom's beauty in thy eyes, where the corners gleam with a reddish glow.[55] Thus he brings the day to an end, as the Creator brings the world to an end when he has doomed all beings to extinction.

[31]   "Thy father's waterfalls have now laid aside their rainbow

diadems, for the setting sun no longer sends his rays upon their spray.

"The little distance which came between the drake and his duck as they swam on the pond has now stretched out into a great one. Both were nibbling at the filaments of one lotus blossom. But now they give this up, they twist their necks around and quack to each other, for they are under the ban of fate.

"The elephants are coming forth from the place where they have spent the day, to drink the water which they need for sustenance from early morn to eve.[56] It is fragrant with many a filament of frankincense trees, and over its surface a swarm of bees are clinging close to the lotus blossoms.

"See, my bashful beloved, how yonder on the western horizon the sun is building a golden bridge with its long drawn out reflection in the water of the lake.

"The boars, defenders of the jungle herds of wild pigs, have already abandoned the little pond with its deep mud, having overcome the heat. As they come forth from it, it looks as if twisted lotus stems which they had bitten off were sticking in their snouts.

"O big-thighed one, this peacock here, sitting on the treetop, his tail-feathers glowing as ruddily as molten gold, is drinking in the glow of the declining twilight.

"The sun has scattered the summer mist, and the darkness spreading over the east makes that part of the sky look like mud. Thus the sky seems like a dried-up pond in which only a little water is left.

"Yonder gazelles are approaching the huts; the roots of the trees are soaked with water poured from pots; sacred cows are coming in to give their milk for the fire offering; the fires are already blazing up: thus do the hermitages put on the appearance of beauty.

"Although the lotus blossom is already closing its petals,

yet it tarries a little while with an opening which still remains, as if it wished to give the bees which delight in it a last quick chance to slip in. It is well fitted, indeed, to be their dwelling place.

"The sunbeams drop down to the horizon from the crimson sun glowing in the western sky, like the filaments of a scarlet cinquefoil with which a maiden has adorned her brow.

[41]   "Yonder the hermits are drinking in the rays of the sun and exalting the sun-god with Vedic hymns, the music of which is enchanting as the neighing of a galloping chariot horse. But he has now transferred his brilliance to the fire.

"This sun-god has lowered the day down into the great ocean, and now goes to rest with his steeds. Their necks are bowed, their hair is in their eyes, and the harness has parted their manes.

"The sun has set. The world is under the spell which lulls it to sleep. It is the glory of the supreme luminary to dazzle the world when he is on high, but to bring sleep as soon as he goes down.

"The twilight follows the divine form of the sun-god, who still tarries on the summit of the western mountain. Should not she, who preceded him in the morning when he ascended, likewise follow after him at his downfall?

"Dearest, with thy gorgeous crown of wavy hair, the wisps of clouds yonder are shining red and yellow and orange. They seem to have been beautifully painted by the evening twilight, as if she had been thinking that thou wouldst be looking at them.

"See yonder how the mountain divides the twilight dusk, as it were, among the manes of the lions, the branches of the trees, and the ruddy mountain peaks.

"The pious hermits, trained in the ritual, now leave the ground to stand on their feet. They pour out the purifying water as an oblation and quietly chant the evening hymn, for they are striving for the expiation of their sins.

"Therefore let me likewise leave thee just for a moment, in order that I too may perform my rites. Sweetly speaking sweetheart, thy two handmaidens will amuse thee meanwhile, for they know plenty of stories."

But the mountain princess pouted, piqued by these words of her husband, and chatted with her handmaiden Vidshaya, who was lying at her side.

Then when the Lord had completed his own evening rites, reciting the sacred mantras, he came back to Parvati, who was very cold and did not say a word. He, however, smiled, and spoke to her as follows:

"Put away thy anger, for thou hast no cause to be angry. [51] It was only the coming of darkness, and no other reason, which called me to my devotions. Dost thou not know that we too are subject to duty, which requires me to act in this way, like a drake?

"The body, my Pretty One, which once upon a time the Self-Existent gave up after the creation of the Fathers, is worshiped as the dawn and twilight. Angry sweetheart, it was only for it that I had regard.

"See, O mountain princess, how this rosy sunset, which is already oppressed by the darkness, glows like a stream laden with red clay and with yellow tamala trees standing at a place on its banks.

"The twilight gleam has disappeared. Only a red streak still marks the western horizon. Thus it is like a battlefield where a bent and bloody sword is lying on the ground.

"But now see, with thy big eyes, how Mount Sumeru has covered the last glimmer of twilight. Pitch darkness spreads through every corner of the sky, all unchecked.

"Nothing can any longer be seen above, or below, or to the side, or before, or behind. At night this world exists as if in a womb, or enclosed in an eggshell created by the darkness.

"What is clear and what is muddy, what is inflexible and what is mobile, what is crooked and what is straight — darkness now makes all to look alike. Alas! There is no longer any distinction! I see only undifferentiated evil!

"But now the moon is coming up to drive away the darkness of the night. See, my lotus-faced bride, the eastern horizon seems as if it were covered with ketaka[57] filaments.

"The night, with her stars and with the moon hiding his orb behind the crest of Mount Mandara, is like unto thee, when thou art with thy handmaidens and with me hiding behind your backs to listen to your words.

"The full moon shows only a feeble smile of moonlight in the east, for he delayed his rising until the day had disappeared. The eastern quarter reveals him reluctantly, as one reveals a secret, because her friend the night was coaxing her to do so.

[61]   "See how yonder the moon, shining like a ripe phalini fruit, appears both in the sky and in the water of the lake, like a drake and his duck, in sight of each other, yet separated.

"The newborn moonbeams are as tender as unripe barley buds. I could break them off with my fingernails and make them into a lovely diadem to crown thy locks.

"The moon, having driven the darkness far away by his beams, seems to be stroking back the black hair of his mistress, the night, with his fingers, and kissing her face, while she closes her eyes, the lotus blossoms, in ecstasy.

"Look, Parvati! The light of the risen moon has put to flight the murky darkness, and the sky is like the waters of Lake Manasa, quiet once more after being roiled by the sportive elephants.

"Now the moon is rid of his reddish glow; he shines pure and white and full. In pure beings a temporary blemish soon comes to an end.

"The moonlight dwells on the high places, but the darkness of night flees to the depths below. The paths of virtue and of vice were so clearly marked out by the Creator that each naturally follows its proper direction.

"The peacocks sleeping here in the trees on the valley slope are awakened by the mountain sooner than their wont, by means of the dewdrops drawn from the moonstones by the moonbeams to fall to the valley below.

"Darling, thou of matchless beauty, it looks to me as if the moon, with his rays shining on the tops of the wishing-trees, were wishing to count all the strings of pearls hanging there.

"As the mountain rises and falls again, so the moonlight alternates with the darkness, like the magic beauty of a rutting elephant adorned with streaks of paint.

"While the buzzing of the bee is heard within it, the lotus bursts open to the very stem, as if it could no longer resist the limpid moonlight, which it drinks in with a sigh.[58]

"See, pouter, how brightly the moon is shining on the gown hanging on yonder wishing-tree. Its form is so vague that it is seen to be a gown only because it is fluttering in the breeze.

[71]

"I could pick up with my fingers these wisps of moonlight which the leaves have broken off and which are as delicate as the flowers which fall from these trees, and entwine them in thy locks.

"Pretty one, the moon is joined with the brightest star, which is round and tremulous, like a bridegroom with a maid just married, whose trembling reveals her nervousness.

"Wife, while thou art gazing at the moon, his light is covering thy cheeks, which are shining as fair as budding sedge and now beaming even more brightly because the moon's reflection lies upon them.

"And now the guardian goddess of the Gandhamadana wood is coming to serve thee, my noble lady, with reverence, bringing us sweet wine from the wishing-tree in a crimson colored vessel made of moonstone.

"Thy mouth is naturally fragrant like the nectar of the flowers, and thy eyes possess a natural redness. Say then, pretty one, what further beauty can this wine produce when thou hast drunk it?

"Or shall, perhaps, thy lovable attendants alone drink all this wine, which inflames the god of love?" Thus did Siva speak lovingly to Parvati, and made her drink.

By drinking this wine she was brought into a condition which was ravishing to the heart, in spite of the alteration it caused. She was like a mango tree suddenly infused with sweet fragrance by the working of some incomprehensible charm.

The fair one now came entirely into the power of Siva and of intoxication. In both of them shame disappeared, longing for the divan arose, and passion flamed up violently in both.

First the Lord drank, but he drank in Uma's face, not yet with his lips but with his eyes. Her eyes were already rolling back and forth, her speech was choked, drops of perspiration fell from her face, and she began to giggle.

[81]   Then Siva took his beloved in his arms. Her gold embroidered belt hung down from her body as he embraced her. Her hips were so heavy that he could hardly carry her. Finally he came into the room, made all of precious stones, which was filled with radiance and splendor by the mere power of his thought.

There, together with his beloved, he ascended the bridal bed, with its bedspread of flamingo-white linen, beautiful as a sandbank on the shore of the Ganges, like the moon-god shining above the white autumnal cloud.

Her locks were scattered, her sandalwood powder was rubbed off, her limbs were marked all over by the scratches of his fingernails, her body glowed with the heat of the struggle, her waistband was torn to pieces. But even such a consummation did not satiate his passion.

It was only from tender regard for his beloved, whose arms were wound around him, that he was willing to go to sleep, when the stars were already beginning to disappear.

But at dawn he, who was used to the hymns of the seers, was greeted with the lilting melody of a carol sung by satyrs. Thus he awoke, along with the golden lotus blossoms.

When the couple's embracing had somewhat relaxed their passion, the breezes brought them their service and homage. They had dexterously broken off the petals of many lotus blossoms, and had stirred up whitecaps on Lake Manasa as they blew across from Gandhamadana.

At this moment Siva was enraptured as his eyes rested upon the rows of scratches which his fingernails had left upon her thighs, and he prevented her when she tried to hold close to her body the garments which were hanging loosely.

Then, as he gazed upon the face of his beloved, whose eyes shone with a reddish light because she had been awake all night, and also observed her disheveled locks and obliterated tilaka, as well as her lips, which had been deeply cut by his teeth, the sight of these only aroused renewed joy in the passionate God.

Through the day and through the night he craved the magic potion on his beloved's lips, which only increased his passion the more. He would not greet those who wanted[59] to see him after so long a time, although announced by Vijaya.

In such manner days and nights passed by, devoted only to the pleasures of love. As the fire which burns at the bottom of the ocean is never extinguished by the flood of waters, so was he never sated with love, but spent a hundred fifty seasons like a single night.

Notes

1   Apsarases, beautiful nymphs, sometimes employed by Indra, king of the gods, to seduce hermits who are becoming powerful through asceticism. The nymph Menaka, sent to seduce the ascetic Visvamitra, became the mother of Sakuntala, heroine of Kalidasa's play *Sakuntala*.

2   The red pearly drops on the temples of elephants in rut are frequently mentioned by Sanskrit poets to add an erotic nuance.

3   The chowry or yak tail is an emblem of royalty.

4   The soma plant, from which the sacrificial wine is made.

5   *Sati* (present participle feminine of the verb to be), literally "Beingess."

6   Her father (Primeval Deity) had insulted her husband (God).

7   *Kama*, Love, depicted as an archer whose arrows are flowers and bowstring a row of bees. Desire (*Rati*) is his wife and Spring his best friend.

8   Literally, like an altar.

9   Kama.

10   For it closes at night.

11   Siva, that is, God.

12   Brahma, another person of God — not to be confused with gods, in the polytheistic sense, of whom Indra is king.

13   The Trinity: Brahma, Vishnu, Siva.

14   God of the sea.

15   God of wealth.

16   God of death.

17   Indra's elephant.

18   Siva. Brahma frequently grants boons to ascetics, usually including invincibility, but always with some small print in the contract by overlooking which the ascetic is eventually destroyed. In Taraka's case the escape clause was a provision that he could not be defeated except by a seven-day-old child.

19   Teacher of the demons.

20   That is, as contrasted with his personified form as a god.

21   The North, ruled by Kuvera, represented as an ugly monster.

22   The usual preliminary to its blossoming according to Sanskrit poets.

23   It was customary to have one's name engraved on his arrows. The mango flower is the bees' delight and Kama's favorite arrow.

24   The decorative mark on the forehead of a Hindu woman, but here a pun, *tilaka* also being a tree.

25   It was customary to cover the lips with beeswax during the winter.

26   An inauspicious planet.

27   For Kalidasa the ultimate in sex appeal is a girl frightened by a bee. In *Sakuntala* the King compares the natural charm of a girl so frightened with the artificial charm of court ladies who pretend to be frightened by bees. It is not quite clear how frightened Parvati really was.

28   That is, all her body hairs stirred with ecstasy, like the filaments of this staminiferous flower.

29   As a sati burned on her husband's funeral pyre.

30   God of justice.

31   And still is — Gaurisankar, in the Himalaya Mountains.

32   Daniel Ingalls (*Anthology of Sanskrit Court Poetry*, p. 28) says: "Uma is the mother-goddess . . . the goddess of earth and fertility. And so her appearance is described as a sort of double, an anthropomorph, of the earth. The steam rises from her silent body just as it rises from the parched earth when the monsoon breaks. The rain courses down her just as it courses over the face of the earth we walk on, softening it and making it able to bear our crops."

33   It was an Indian belief that ducks, although greatly devoted to their mates, are under a compulsion to spend the night on opposite sides of the stream.

34   That is, an incarnation of religious study. A Hindu of high caste should spend his life first as a student, then as a householder, then as a hermit, finally as a mendicant.

35   Virtue, pleasure, and prosperity.

36   Ascetic merit is transferable, but she misses the hidden meaning: he offers her half of himself, and only then will he know himself.

37   This need not mean that these great gods had been actively wooing her; in a polygynous society a princess can usually marry whomever she will.

38   Wife of Vasishtha, one of the Seers, and a model of wifely virtue.

39   Vishnu, incarnate as a boar, held the earth above the flood at this crisis.

40   The converse analogy is proposed by Gaston Bachelard, who, in his *La Psychanalyse du Feu*, argues that making fire by rubbing-sticks is essentially and originally a sexual act.

41   The sacred river arises from Vishnu's foot, flows through Siva's hair and across heaven, falls in a cataract upon Himalaya, and thence flows through India to the sea.

42   Vishnu incarnate as a dwarf begged the demon Bali for three paces of land, but then grew to such a size that they covered the entire universe.

43   Hindu mythologists and artists sometimes represent them as having a single body.

44   Some of these worthies ride on bulls, others on owls.

45   Kali, Goddess in her terrible aspect, here represented with poetic license as a separate personality.

46   Yak-tail chowries, like the umbrella a symbol of royalty, fluttering in the hands of the personified rivers like swans over the surface of the actual rivers.

47   The poet was so pleased with these six couplets that he repeated them verbatim, in a suitable context, in his other epic poem *The Race of Raghu.*

48   Because the crowds of women pressed so close to Siva that the rice ritually thrown on him struck their bracelets.

49   Goddess of Beauty, wife of Vishnu.

50   Goddess of Wisdom and Eloquence, wife of Brahma.

51   That is, in the vernacular. Parvati, being a woman, would not be expected to understand Sanskrit.

52   I do not understand this phrase, unless it is some kind of flower.

53   Frightened, I take it, by the roaring of wild animals on Mount Kailasa.

54   Wife of Indra and queen of the gods.

55   The sun, still brilliant as a golden lotus in the center, is getting red around the periphery.

56   Elephants drink once a day, at sunset.

57   The very fragrant, white-flowered "screw pine."

58   Here, as often, two ideas seem to be mingled in the poet's imagination: the lotus which is the dwelling place of the bees, described above as closing at sunset, and a different species which blossoms at night. Compare the verse in *Sakuntala,* "The moon opens the night flower, and the sun makes the water lily blossom; each is confined to its own object, and thus a virtuous man abstains from any connection with the wife of another."

59   Reading *wollten* for *wollte.*

Design and typesetting by
Typo/Graphics, Mystic, Connecticut
Set in Aldine Roman with Cantos opened in Heritage
Running heads are Theme